We are often told that hard times bring  It
would be good if that were true, but if yc k
coming that can help you. *Sustainability ir* -
ties can help to make the cuts that reall |
waste.

Ed Mayo, Secretary General, (...............~ un, and co-author of
Consumer Kids

A beautifully useful book.

Professor Paul James, Director,
UN Global Compact Cities Programme

Whilst we have faced periods of austerity before in the UK, the current predic-
ament combines widespread pressure on investment and economic activity
with the urgent environmental need to move to a sustainable future. This publication for local authorities provides a vision for a cost-neutral drive towards
sustainable outcomes, illustrated with examples of workable and practical
initiatives that inspire and motivate the changes we need.

David Nussbaum, Chief Executive, WWF-UK

Beyond the gestures of the great and the good, Philip Monaghan has identified
a treasure trove buried in the devilish details of the local, driven by unsung
heroes, that will be the currency of sustainability in an era of austerity.

Simon Zadek, Visiting Senior Fellow, Harvard's J F Kennedy School for
Government, Senior Advisor on Sustainability to the World Economic
Forum, and author of the award-winning book *The Civil Corporation*

Local authorities and the communities they serve must be at the forefront
of sustainability. This book provides practical insight on achieving a better
environment and stronger society with limited resources—essential reading
for all leaders working in local government.

Martin Baxter, Executive Director—Policy, Institute of Environmental
Management and Assessment

Whilst 'doing more with less' may appear an obvious and simple course of
action to take, the reality is that it can still falter badly if not approached in a
strategic way that is aligned to high-level, core business issues and everyday
operational systems. The great value of Philip Monaghan's book is that it fully
recognises this, building the business case first, then showing what practical
interventions to make, backed up with real-life examples, and tailoring it all
for local government managers challenged with advancing sustainability in a
new age of austerity.

Peter Lacy, Partner & Managing Director, Accenture Sustainability
Services. Europe. Africa. Middle East and Latin America

Too often, the literature for strategies on how to address the complexities of ensuring the future sustainability of our communities is targeted towards our global leaders, the business world or the consumer. Very little research has been aimed at the local policy-makers and civil servants who face the on-the-ground challenges of delivering sustainable solutions for our future through policy, programmes and delivery. The author has now closed that gap with a well-written and thoughtful look at practical approaches from Kyoto to Knowsley which reflect the realities of public spending cuts, yet provide answers and case studies that local governments can learn from.

Bill Boler, Director, Physical Regeneration,
Business in the Community

Developing economies in particular, have unique challenges in 'doing more with less'. Service delivery at local level where capacity and resource constraints are immanent, remains a crucial ingredient in developing sustainable future societies. Therefore, finding creative and workable solutions in dealing with this is urgently needed. This book indeed provides such solutions specifically for (responsible) leaders in local governments and will play a vital role in the drive towards sustainable future societies. A must-read!

Professor Derick de Jongh, Director, Centre for Responsible Leadership,
University of Pretoria

Have we ever needed Philip Monaghan's invitation to experience the kaleidoscope of cost-neutral ways towards sustainability more than now? . . . Monaghan does not leave us any reason to fail to act. He clearly shows that it is absolutely possible for local governments to battle for sustainable development at low cost or no cost while creating win–win situations. While looking at cities around the world, he has collected numerous practical examples from outside the box that can now serve as blueprints for local leaders. As our economies are on the mend, it might be easier to pick these up. The next depression is waiting around the corner, while climate change turns out to be progressively aggressive! An encouraging book and recommended reading for mayors and councillors.

Holger Robrecht, Director, Sustainability Management Programme,
ICLEI—Local Governments for Sustainability

A readable and inspiring book which will guide local councils around the world to do more with less and leave a better planet for our grandchildren.

Professor Carol Adams, Pro-Vice Chancellor (Sustainability),
La Trobe University, Melbourne

This book is about smart solutions. Drawing on examples from across the world, it shows how those public sector organisations at the sharp end of delivery can get bigger sustainability outcomes with less money.

Peter Madden, Chief Executive, Forum for the Future

Inspiring and very readable, *Sustainability in Austerity* is the essential guide to the local solutions that work.

Alex MacGillivray, Director, AccountAbility

Sustainability in Austerity

Philip Monaghan

SUSTAINABILITY IN AUSTERITY
How Local Government Can Deliver During Times of Crisis

Greenleaf
PUBLISHING

© 2011 Greenleaf Publishing Limited

Published by Greenleaf Publishing Limited
Aizlewood's Mill
Nursery Street
Sheffield S3 8GG
UK
www.greenleaf-publishing.com

Printed in Great Britain on acid-free paper by CPI Antony Rowe, Chippenham, Wiltshire

FSC
www.fsc.org
MIX
Paper from
responsible sources
FSC® C013604

Cover by LaliAbril.com

British Library Cataloguing in Publication Data:
    A catalogue record for this book is available from the British Library.
    ISBN-13: 978-1-906093-57-0

This book is dedicated to my Mum and Dad.

You shamed and framed me into the person I am by being 'local heroes'; and even though you're not around to see the results, thank you for giving me your grit and your wits.

Contents

The 102 cost-neutral interventions

Case studies

Anecdotes

Management tips

Figures, tables and boxes

Tables

Boxes

Preface

- Why is it fundamentally important for leaders in local government to 'play to win' when it comes to sustainability?

- What practical action can councils take to implement national policies at a time when budgets are being savagely cut?

- Why is the need to improve sustainability performance ever more urgent, yet public appetite for change is on the wane?

This book seeks to bring forward answers to all these questions and more.

With tremendous wits and determination we can battle back and take 'game-changing' action on sustainable matters, even as we try to recover from a horrific global recession. But to do so, we must continually make change desirable, whether in relation to tackling poverty, obesity or climate change. This is the great challenge faced by leaders in local government who are at the forefront of this sustainability effort, given the critical role these municipal authorities play in delivering public services.

For many, local councils are pivotal to the delivery of sustainability as every aspect of their role shapes how people live their lives—from democratic elections to education, and planning to waste collection.

I am constantly amazed by the passion and commitment shown by public servants to help the communities they serve, from Caracas and Liverpool to Maryland and Melbourne. My motivation for writing this book is to share inspirational insights from around the world into how leaders in local government can continue to advance good sustainability practices in such austere times.

The idea for this book emerged in 2009 during the international bailout of a number of private banks to avoid full-scale system failure. As the crisis unfolded it became very apparent that the huge mountains of debt being built up by central governments was unsustainable and that cuts would need to be made to balance the books—and, more importantly, that the public sector would be one of the first in line when the axe was to start swinging. Yet this was at the very same time that green advocates from business, academia and civil society were making calls for greater investment at the local level in big issues of the day, such as limiting consumption to counter a growing world population or making the transition to a low-carbon economy.

So, in essence, leaders in local government are going to be asked to do a lot more but with much less money! To make matters worse, increasing public scepticism about why we should deal with these dilemmas in the first place has exacerbated the problem, notably concerns over the robustness of the science of climate change.

There is no need to be defeatist, however. Humankind has faced and defeated worse situations before: the plague, world wars and terrorism. We have battled back before and can do the same again.

Indeed, a crisis can often provide an opportunity for accelerating new, bold ideas or actions on massive dilemmas such as these.

Given this, it seemed to me that a compendium of cost-neutral and powerful ways for leaders in local government to save the planet was needed. That is, innovative self-help methods achieved through habit-forming behaviour change among council members, staff and local communities alike. Provided in this book are the required rules of leadership, and relevant case studies, anecdotes and management tips derived from a wealth of learning by like-minded peers across the world, all of whom have faced and overcome serious sustainability challenges.

One year on and the book is now on the shelves. Wonderful insights include primary case interview research with local government leaders in Caracas (Venezuela), Ekurhuleni (South Africa), Fort Chipewyan (Canada), Krakow (Poland), Merseyside (UK), Montgomery (USA),

Nillumbik (Australia) and Ulaanbaatar (Mongolia), as well as many others.

It has been a fantastic journey thus far for me and I hope it is as helpful to you in your work as is it is for me in mine.

This is not the end of the story, though. Please do share your own insights with me at sustainabilityinausterity.wordpress.com, where you can find the latest tips through my ongoing learning exchange with others.

Philip Monaghan
September 2010

Acknowledgements

It is important to acknowledge a number of key people who have generously contributed to this book.

First, thank you to Eve Sadler who has been so supportive throughout the whole writing and editing process, and who is the kind and brave soul who painstakingly reviewed the early manuscript draft.

For the provision of insightful case studies, sincere thanks go to George Poitras, Lino Clemente, Margaret Abbey, Douglas Weisburger, Wieslaw Starowicz, Agata Mierzyńska, Malgorzata Mrugala, John Flaherty, Dee Pilane, Stephanie McCarthy and Paul James.

With regard to ideas for management tips, anecdotes and for sharing fantastic contacts from their networks, my appreciation goes to Jonathan Cohen, Jason Perks, Aiden Cohen, Paul Monaghan, Ed Mayo, Rowena Soriaga, Karen Lawrence, Maya Roy, Philip Hughes, Carol Adams, Derick de Jongh, Eben Le Roux, Barbara Schnitzer, Steve Connor, Eddy Buranakul, Johan Nel, Alejandro Litovsky, Fabiola Aranda and Jennifer Watson.

Finally, my gratitude goes to all the team at Greenleaf Publishing and in particular John Stuart for backing this project; to Catherine Monaghan for producing some amazing artwork as well as insightful management tips; and to Joe Monaghan for counselling me on the brave new world of multimedia publishing.

So, a million thank yous to one and all!

Part I
THE DENTIST'S CHAIR

1

Why you should read this book

National governments have their national [sustainability] policies, but after all it is local governments who have to implement these policies (UN Secretary General, Ban Ki-moon 2009).

1.1 **Establishing need**

While developed and developing economies alike are slowly emerging from the worst recession since the USA's first Great Depression at the start of the last century, the turmoil of the recovery is likely to last for years to come. The massive debt burden on national governments in the West from the various bank bailouts has caused a ripple effect that has been felt across the world. One consequence of this emergency response to the economic devastation is a dramatic and virtually unanimous reduction on public spending in the medium to long term, even if some are still implementing a short-term spending stimulus to avert further recession.

This has created a 'perfect storm' in local governments whereby the public's expectations and national targets on sustainability issues are increasing at the same time as funds are being drastically cut. Therefore, this is a major challenge for anyone associated with a local authority. One example is the costly commitments to establish targets to reduce greenhouse gas (GHG) emissions under the Copenhagen Accord, which have come at the height of the crisis (UNFCCC 2010).

Given this financial straitjacket, this book is a must-read for all council leaders in need of advice on cost-neutral actions and to equip you to 'do more for less'. Filling this vast gap in know-how is the key achievement of this book. This is done through primary as well as secondary research, including new critical insights from case interviews with local government leaders from across Africa, Asia–Pacific, Europe, Latin America and North America. Sharing reflections from a new generation of public service innovators will assist the drive towards excellence on sustainability in defiance of the credit crunch.

More specifically, this book is intended to inform and inspire a range of managers in local government working to improve the lives of the communities you serve, as well as the elected members who lead our councils, shaping strategy and holding managers to account for performance. Crucially, the book is not aimed at the converted but rather is intended to persuade and support all council leaders who control or influence the use of natural, financial, human and other assets. This includes more traditional services ranging from economic development and planning to fleet and logistics, and is structured to be most helpful to such a particular reader.

For the first time in a generation, public servants and elected councillors have a critical window of opportunity to engage in new forms of learning and innovation that may actually lay the foundations to increase your council's competitiveness—are you ready to make the 'upside of down' a reality?

1.2 **A review of other literature**

There is an impressive array of books that provide fresh thinking on sustainability, ranging from major public policy shifts to step-by-step guidance on the implementation of environmental management standards or to mentoring on personal well-being. However, these tend to be aimed at policy-makers in national government and not leaders in local government who are the ones that have to make this change a reality, as appears to be the case for *Plan B 4.0* (Brown 2009), *Deep Economy* (McKibben 2010) and *Leading Change Toward Sustainability* (Doppelt 2010). Or, the target readers are executives from big business such as with *Business and Economic Development* (Monaghan *et al.* 2003) and *Corporate Environmental Management* (Welford 1997). Or, the advice is aimed at individual domestic audiences such as *Sustainability by Design* (Ehrenfeld 2010), *The Economical Environmentalist* (Vaze 2009) and *Change the World for a Fiver* (We Are What We Do 2007). Crucially, these publications have ignored or overlooked the inclusion of inspirational stories of positive change from peers in local government. More importantly, as public sector budgets are slashed, neither are they contextualised by the need to act in a cost-neutral way.

Furthermore, there are also trade associations or partnership forums serving the public sector which provide insightful policy briefings or propose some practical actions on sustainability-related legislation among other things. Impressive examples include the UN Global Compact Cities Programme (e.g. *Sustainable Cities*, Volume 1 2010), C40 Cities Group led by the Clinton Foundation in the USA, the European Covenant of Mayors, the UK's Local Government Association (e.g. *The Climate Challenge* 2009) and Forum for the Future (e.g. *The Sustainable Cities Index* 2009a) as well as the ICLEI: Local Governments for Sustainability. However, as with the literature above while these are extremely helpful, they are not intended to provide council leaders with practical, cost-neutral advice which is most needed during these austere times.

More information and signposting to several of these respected organisations and other initiatives such as ICLEI or the UN Global Compact Cities Programme are detailed in the section 'Other helpful sources of learning'.

Consequently, all of the above evidence has helped to inform the focus and layout of the book. That is, it allows you to understand and implement the interventions on your own terms, while supporting you and your teams to coordinate tangible and lasting organisation-wide change on sustainability.

1.3 **How to use this resource**

The primary target readers here are managers and councillors in local government across the world—in either emerging or developed economies. A secondary audience is managers in central government, community organisation leaders, academics and management consultants who work with this sector on policy and performance.

More specifically, for traditional public services it will be relevant to the disciplines listed below:

- Democracy and decision-making (constitutional roles, scrutiny, innovation and transparency)

- Corporate assets and resources (finance, procurement, estates management and personnel)

- Economic development and planning (land use, business incubation and jobs and skills)

- Waste and environmental services (waste reduction, re-use and recycling)

- Fleet and logistics (staff travel, business travel and public travel)

- Community management (localism and neighbourhood participation, education and well-being)

The book is divided into four parts. Part I, 'The dentist's chair', talks about our fear and motivation to act on the big sustainability issues of the day. In Part II, 'Doing much more with a lot less', the discussion is then further contextualised in terms of the global credit crunch and its crippling impact on local government spending. Part III, 'The upside of down with amazing people', sets out a series of cost-neutral initiatives that you, as leaders in local government, can take during these difficult times. Following this, Part IV, 'Out of the darkness: golden rules for excellence in austerity', argues that, in order to realise these opportunities for sustainable living, certain organisational enablers need to be in place for us to battle back and reach the promised land.

Over 100 case studies, anecdotes and practical tips for managers and councillors from their peers across the globe aim to help you build the business case that cost-neutral change is within our grasp. Fortunately, this does not mean starting with a blank piece of paper. Rather, it is about building on existing successes as a clear path to organisational excellence. It involves aligning activities to strategic intent and operational systems and understanding the trade-offs and related risks. All of which is explored in more detail during the course of the book. (For ease of comparability all financial values are calculated in US dollars.)

To help you navigate your way through this learning resource Figure 1.3 illustrates a high-level 'route map'.

This figure shows how the chapters are brigaded together into four distinct parts and 'where you are now' in your reading journey (so, given you are currently reading Part I this is highlighted accordingly). Then within each of these four parts, at the beginning of the relevant chapters (2, 3, 5 and 7–15), you will be able to refer to summary tables which list all 'cost-neutral interventions' associated with 'typical sustainability actions and outcomes' for that particular section (note that the long list of over 100 interventions are numbered at the start of the book). An example of a summary table is shown in Table 1.3 (taken from Chapter 9 'Economic development and planning').

TABLE 1.3 **Example of a summary table**

Typical sustainability actions and outcomes	Cost-neutral interventions
Land use and climate adaptation	#5, #66, #22
Low-carbon trade zones	#23, #67
Business incubation, signals and control	#68, #69, #70, #24
Green space infrastructure	#71, #25

And then, finally, at the end of each chapter, the 'Key learning' is all brought together.

So, regardless of whether you are a seasoned professional or just starting out in sustainability, this book is written to be an invaluable resource tailored to the challenges you are facing, as suggested below.

FIGURE 1.3 **Route mapping**

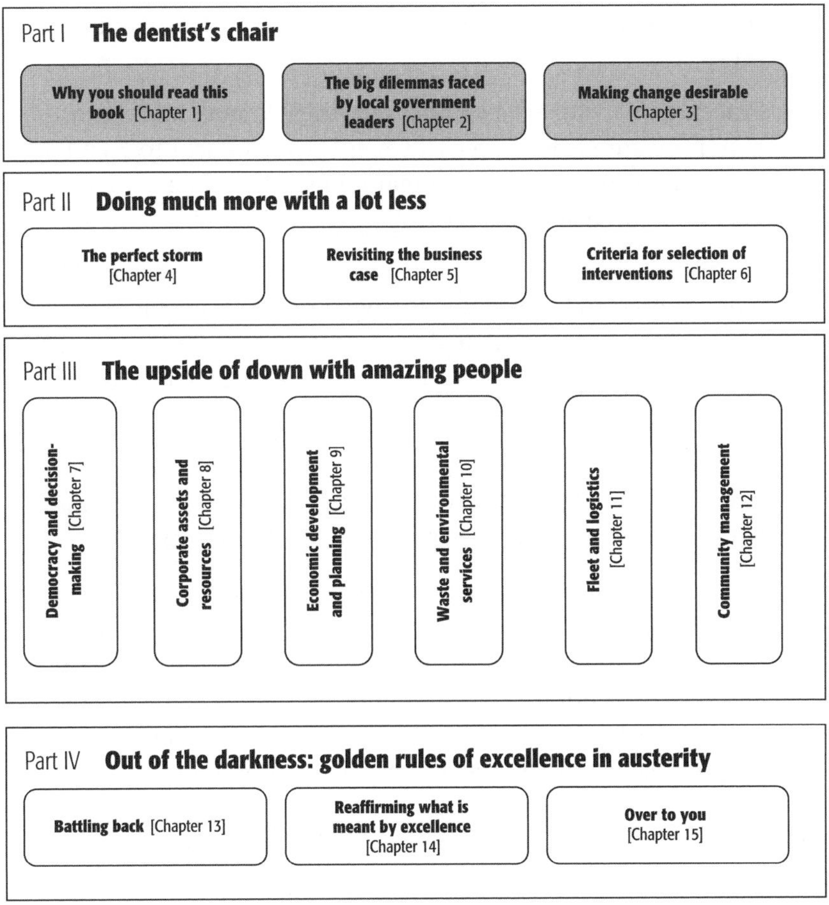

Part I **The dentist's chair**

| **Why you should read this book** [Chapter 1] | **The big dilemmas faced by local government leaders** [Chapter 2] | **Making change desirable** [Chapter 3] |

Part II **Doing much more with a lot less**

| **The perfect storm** [Chapter 4] | **Revisiting the business case** [Chapter 5] | **Criteria for selection of interventions** [Chapter 6] |

Part III **The upside of down with amazing people**

| **Democracy and decision-making** [Chapter 7] | **Corporate assets and resources** [Chapter 8] | **Economic development and planning** [Chapter 9] | **Waste and environmental services** [Chapter 10] | **Fleet and logistics** [Chapter 11] | **Community management** [Chapter 12] |

Part IV **Out of the darkness: golden rules of excellence in austerity**

| **Battling back** [Chapter 13] | **Reaffirming what is meant by excellence** [Chapter 14] | **Over to you** [Chapter 15] |

- For the more experienced practitioner who is primarily interested in the case studies or management tips, the list of the 100 cost-neutral interventions will direct you quickly to these

- Practitioners who are beginners to the field may wish to take it step by step from cover to cover through Part I to Part IV. Or perhaps focus on a particular council function; if so, Part III is structured accordingly

- For those who wish to refresh their learning or are possibly more interested in revisiting the power of their business case to act as part of 'competing' for scarce resources, Part II will be helpful in building the persuasiveness and stickiness of your programmes

- If you are primarily intrigued by management theory and models, then Part IV is the best place to spend your time, before checking back to earlier sections of the book

- Furthermore, if you are skilled in a particular discipline, you may simply wish to look at how you incorporate sustainability thinking into your day job. If so, again start with Part III and select the appropriate chapters: for instance, if you work in personnel or finance, then begin with the chapter on 'Corporate assets and resources', and take it from there

- If you are an academic you may simply want to focus your time on the case studies compiled from primary research, with interviews from Africa, Asia, Europe, Latin America and North America. Again, these are listed in the 100 interventions

- Finally, if you are a business person looking at ideas for ways to partner with local authorities, you may find it useful to flick through the numerous anecdotes, particularly those related to 'Economic development and planning' or 'Waste and environmental services', again contained in Part III

Key learning

✓ This book aims to fill a hole in the available advice on practical, cost-neutral ways for local government to improve sustainability performance.

✓ The target audience is primarily council managers and elected members from authorities around the world.

✓ This book is structured in a way that will assist established service providers such as finance or fleet in making the best use of this learning resource.

2

The big dilemmas faced by local government leaders

Help us to help you ... without local action, there is no global solution (Councillor Gary Porter, Chair, Local Government Association of England and Wales' Environment Board 2009).

Typical sustainability actions and outcomes	Cost-neutral interventions
2.1 Dental hygiene	–
2.2 The vital role of local government	#9, #10
2.3 Clarifying how we define 'sustainability'	–

2.1 **Dental hygiene**

There is general consensus in the international scientific community that we are severely challenged with adapting to a more sustainable livelihood. For some this means consuming less as an affluent society, while for others who are less well off it might mean having to do more to sustain life itself.

Despite this, in terms of dealing with the perils of poverty, climate change or obesity, it feels for many like 'going to the dentist'. None of us really wants to do it, yet we know it is important and, generally, we end up feeling better afterwards. However, just like a trip to the dentist, it is not cheap to do, and the longer we put it off the worse it gets, even if the benefits are great.

So, for our local government leaders, moving away from an unsustainable way of living, working or playing should really be about a primary duty of care to protect our communities. By adapting to more sustainable living we can help improve quality of life, tackle poverty, create new jobs and secure energy or food supply, as well as future-proofing ourselves against dramatic changes in weather conditions or population demographics.

Thus, just like a visit to the dentist, it is always wise for us to act early, even when an apparent lack of desirability impedes our ability to take the necessary action. Local government has a crucial role to play in smashing this barrier to force real and positive change (discussed further in Chapter 3).

Before doing this, it is important to remind ourselves of the critical role that local government plays in all our lives. Too often we take it for granted and overlook its vital service.

2.2 The vital role of local government

For many national advocates, such as the Center for a New American Dream or the Korea Research Institute for Human Settlements, local councils are seen as pivotal to the delivery of sustainable development. According to *Stepping Up* (Forum for the Future 2010), every aspect of this role—ranging from democratic elections to education, land use planning and waste management—shapes how people live their lives. If leaders in local government do not take on the challenges afforded to them through their respective national duties and powers, then it is unlikely our communities can adapt to sustainable lifestyles.

Sustainability can strengthen local society and create public value in a number of ways; notably by addressing market failure, building resilience and renewing the social contract (Forum for the Future 2010).

In terms of market failure, local government intervenes to provide goods or services the market is unable or unwilling to offer at a certain price or volume (for example, public transport in remote or isolated rural areas). With regard to resilience, local government develops capabilities and capacity to insulate its vulnerable communities from shock or stress during a crisis to ensure business continuity (for example emergency planning during times of severe weather such as in areas located in high-risk zones for flooding or bushfire). In respect of the social contract, whether written or unwritten, this sets out the rights and responsibilities between the local state and its network of citizens, civil society organisations and businesses (for

---

BOX 2.2 **A new green deal?**

In a global review of stimulus packages, Bendell and Cohen (2009) provide discourse on how green stimulus plans have been hailed in many quarters as the 'New Green Deal', akin to President Roosevelt's fiscal boost to drag the USA out of the Great Crash of the 1920s.

In total, US$2.8 trillion has been set aside for national stimulus plans by states across the world. Investment has been focused on: renewable energy electricity grids, mass transit, low-carbon vehicles, building efficiency, environmental conservation, education, healthcare and the restructuring of tax and financial incentives. Of these countries, most commentators agree that South Korea was one of the more impressive contributors, with 81% or US$31 billion of the entire stimulus plan dedicated to green investments.

In addition to helping to deliver these plans, Bendell and Cohen also consider there to be a key role for local government in corporate governance owing to the scale of deficit-financed spending and the potential threat of bankruptcy and corruption. Consequently, China has announced the deployment of inspection teams to monitor all aspects of stimulus spending in relation to planning, procurement construction and quality, while the US Recovery Act Accountability and Transparency Board was established to conduct oversight of recovery spending, too.

example it provides the foundation for establishing trustworthy and legitimate neighbourhood groups).

Numerous local councils accept this imperative and have been trying to advance a suite of policies accordingly, as demonstrated by case studies and other anecdotes contained throughout this book from Caracas (Venezuela), Ekurhuleni (South Africa), Fort Chipewyan (Canada), Krakow (Poland), Merseyside (UK), Montgomery (USA), Nillumbik (Australia) and Ulaanbaatar (Mongolia), as well as many others.

This pivotal role is further reflected in the fact that a major implication of the global financial crisis is sometimes the return of a hands-on role for the state. This is evident in so-called 'stimulus packages' which have led to increased duties for some local authorities on sustainable matters. Stimulus packages that have a significant green focus are a concept explored in more detail in Box 2.2.

The unique role of local councils was also called on in the recent past for particular sector- and location-specific interventions. Take, for instance, attempts to resolve the difficulties in managing Asian forestry through innovative social networks or so-called landscape alliances (Soriaga 2008).

[#9] **Landscape alliances: local natural resource management in the Philippines**

According to the Asia Forest Network, local governments are faced with the opportunity and challenge to mobilise local networks of 'landscape alliances' in order to manage forestry problems in Cambodia, Indonesia, the Philippines, Thailand and Vietnam. In the Philippines the 1991 Local Government Code devolved a number of functions to provincial municipal and barangay (village) governments including the provision of basic services and some natural resource responsibilities (Soriaga 2008). The informal collectives may simply take on the form of a stakeholder forum or technical working group, offering cost-neutral interventions for potentially huge gain. While many local councils were ill-prepared to take on this decentralised responsibility, alliance-building elsewhere allowed local social movements to deal with natural resource management not covered by national programmes, which led to improved livelihoods and the return of biodiversity.

The Philippines is not alone in calling on the unique role of local government. There have been other, similar, challenging but inspirational actions by councils in South Africa focused on green education to combat crime, improve diets and conserve water.

[#10] **Green education: improving livelihoods in South Africa**

The North-West University's (Du Plessis *et al.* 2004) evaluation of medium-sized local authorities in the southern South African development community (South Africa, Mozambique, Namibia and Swaziland) illustrated the value of simple education measures to inform greener governance. As part of wider funded programmes, this involved the realisation of a number of cost-neutral benefits derived from improved awareness and cooperation with local partners. This included crime prevention through ecodesign by uMhlathuze Local Municipality, water savings by eradicating invader plant species by Klerksdorp Local Municipality and healthier eating from vegetable gardening by Mbombela Local Municipality.

What is clear from both barangay (villages) in the Philippines or from Klerksdorp is that local authorities recognise there is a special role to play and are fighting hard to improve the livelihoods of the citizens they serve, despite the grave challenges they face. (Note being equipped to fulfil one's role is a common theme of both the Asia Forest Network and the North-West University anecdotes and capacity development is fully explored in Part III.)

2.3 Clarifying how we define 'sustainability'

Next, clarification is sought on our interpretation of the term 'sustainability', as this will frame a number of other discussions brought forward in the book. So, although we have seen in Section 2.2 that local government has a vital role to play in advancing sustainable solutions, it is important to understand what we mean by sustainability per se.

The term 'sustainability' has different meanings for different people. Just like all language. However, being clear about its meaning has implications for what we expect, desire to achieve and so on. Regardless of your point of departure or motives, what is clear is that, first, the debate about sustainability is mostly unavoidable and that, second, in considering solutions to the challenge at hand we need to navigate the complex set of interactions between various issues when considering solutions.

In terms of the former, Boulding (1966) refers to this as something like the final 'frontier'. That is, there is nowhere else to run to from the problems humankind has created from unsustainable living and so we must face up to this dilemma and find a solution. With respect to the latter, Perman *et al.* (2003) emphasise the relationship between the 'three sustainabilities' of human development, the natural environment and the economy. Thus, one necessary condition for a society to be sustainable is that its natural environment should be maintained.

Having said all of that, there are literally hundreds of definitions of sustainability in circulation and use! This book does not intend to add to this long list and instead refers to the most popular definition coined in the Brundtland Commission report, which proposes that for development to be sustainable it should: 'meet the needs of the present without comprising the ability of future generations to meet their own needs' (WCED 1987).

This, however, is just the beginning of the debate, and other issues also need to be clarified in the interpretation of this definition. Starting with terminology, what issues—economic, environmental and/ or social—does this actually cover? For instance, in terms of governance, who determines who benefits and who does not with regard to different populations and generations? With regard to legal status, is the concept voluntary in nature or obligatory in law? In respect of performance, is a desired outcome prescribed or are only general principles observed?

For local councils, there may well be many commonalities in such definitions, so the headline cross-cutting issues that might be covered are illustrated in Figure 2.3.

FIGURE 2.3 **Interrelated sustainability aspects**

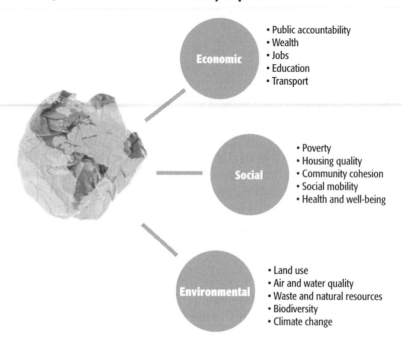

The answer to all these questions is also likely to vary according each one's particular context. That is, it is a matter of what is most relevant or 'material' at any particular moment (Zadek and Merme 2003) and this resulting dilemma may involve dealing with tensions and trade-offs. Key then is that your approach to sustainability is integrated. Take for example your council's management of green space infrastructure (explored further in Section 9.4); it is important here to consider the wider role of, say, forestry in terms of support for the rural economy and urban cooling or flood defence as well as biodiversity or leisure. Furthermore, a dilemma may also mature over time according to your understanding and ability which, in turn, informs an organisation's ability to respond. So, for instance, taking the issue of climate change as a prime example, a sufficiently coherent response to the issue a decade ago might have been for a local council to organise a public debate on the topic with its peers to learn more about the science; now, many councils may be expected to have a climate change mitigation and adaptation strategy in place which sets targets for carbon reduction as a minimum.

If all this holds true, deciding how best to optimise your options on sustainability can then be framed by a consideration of a number of factors such as survivability, consumption patterns or a decent standard of living, and theory of justice or equity as espoused by Rawls (1971) and Hartwick (1977), respectively. Concepts such as fairness and social justice are crucial, as they influence how desirable change is to people (this is explored in Chapter 3).

Key learning

✓ There is general consensus on the need to move away from an unsustainable way of living and we need to overcome the barriers to change.

✓ Local government has a unique role to play in advancing the sustainability debate, as a provider of life-critical public services.

✓ While you may have a different interpretation of sustainability from your peers, there will be commonalities, too, and so the key is understanding what is material to your council given your particular circumstances and how you can manage sustainability in an integrated way.

3

Making change desirable

A critical mass of citizens and businesses is ready and
waiting to act on the challenge of sustainable consumption. But to act, they need the confidence that they will
not be acting alone and against the grain and to no purpose (UK Sustainable Development Commission 2009).

Typical sustainability actions and outcomes	Cost-neutral interventions
3.1 Speaking with sceptics	–
3.2 Bridging the fairness gap	–
3.3 Habit-forming behaviour change	#1

3.1 **Speaking with sceptics**

When the controversy over leaked emails from the University of East
Anglia raged around the world in 2009 during the run up to the UN Climate Summit in Copenhagen, it seemed to damage so many people's
belief that climate change science was real and the problem urgent. A
study by the Pew Research Center found that belief that global warming is occurring dropped from 71% to 56% year-on-year 2008 to 2009
(McKie 2010; Gore and Hodgson 2010). In stark contrast, in previous

years scientists were riding a wave of public trust in comparison with the media and others about climate change as Figure 3.1.1 demonstrates (Forstater *et al.* 2007). This raises many questions. First, why did the public view turn so quickly? Second, why, in many observers' eyes, was subsequent news of the exoneration in 2010 of the researchers at the heart of the story largely ignored? Is it perhaps that the science *was* flawed and it remains wrong for many? Or, is it because bad news is of primary interest to the media? Or, does it owe more to the fact that a powerful fossil fuel lobby may have an inappropriate influence on the political debate?

FIGURE 3.1.1 **How much people in the USA and UK trust different parties on information on climate change**

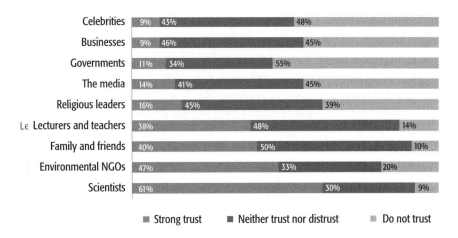

Source: Forstater *et al.* 2007

One or a combination of these reasons may or may not hold true. However, maybe it is because people wanted climate change not to be true, regardless of the data, so they would have an excuse not to take potentially difficult corrective action. Is it just easier because they prefer to be a denialist? (Shermer *et al.* 2010). It is surprising how little time has been devoted to considering this in the ensuing post-scandal discussion: that is, understanding why some ideas survive while others die (Heath and Heath 2007). Indeed, in order to ensure an idea such as the existence of climate change does survive, how does one speak with sceptics to persuade them to agree with this particular point of view (Weiser and Zadek 2000; Borg 2007)?

For the avoidance of doubt, the point of departure for this book is that climate change chaos is real, is manmade (as evidenced by the Intergovernmental Panel on Climate Change's Fourth Assessment Report 2007) but that it is a solvable problem if we act with tremendous grit and with our wits about us and do so immediately.

However, what the scientific community lost sight of during the climate conspiracy is that persuasion is an art not a science. Regurgitating even more climate data about Himalayan glaciers when people have lost trust in them as a reliable source and then arguing about the content of the data or claiming there is a counter-conspiracy at play here is not useful. What would have been helpful is an authoritative source explaining a concrete argument to people in a compelling and sincere, but simple, way. This story should have been both emotive and informative, and ultimately it needed a positive result for the sceptic by securing a good outcome (e.g. reducing household energy bills) or avoiding a bad one (e.g. health concerns arising from emissions). This is depicted in Figure 3.1.2, adapted from Weiser and Zadek (2000) as it was originally intended for a blue-chip audience.

FIGURE 3.1.2 **Persuading sceptics to take a positive decision**

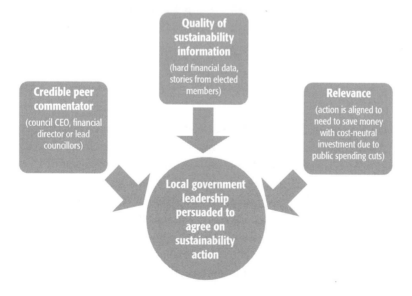

Source: Based on Weiser and Zadek 2000

So, for example, one way to re-run the climate argument might be for locally elected members, business leaders, trade unions and others to come together:

> Reducing our carbon footprint in our local authority is good news for everyone. It means if we are more efficient with our energy consumption that there is less burden on the public purse and therefore our residents' household budgets. If we develop locally generated renewable energy this makes us less reliant on unstable overseas sources, and if we invest in new low-carbon technologies such as electric vehicles or wind turbines, we can up-skill and employ more local people. And, if we reduce emissions arising from our burning of fossil fuels it means our air will be cleaner to breathe and our water cleaner to drink for our children and families. At the same time we also need to make new arrangements to better protect ourselves from any severe and unpredictable weather including flooding or heatwaves. But, to do even a small part of this or for us to start reaping these important benefits we—government, businesses, local communities and citizens—need to 'do our bit'. So, this is why we need to tackle climate change together.

More convincing, right? In short, it is *desirable* for two reasons. First, it touches on close-to-home tangible issues of health, security and employment, yes. Second, and more fundamentally, it is desirable for one other reason in particular. It is fair. How you bridge this fairness gap is considered next.

3.2 Bridging the fairness gap

Perhaps understandably, fairness is at the heart of lots of human choice. The UK's National Consumer Council and Sustainable Development Commission (2009) conclude that when citizens take positive action on sustainability matters it is commonly underpinned by an 'I will if you will' mentality. That is, the public want to see their government, businesses and their community leaders all 'doing their bit', too. In fact, this is what assures us that we can indeed come together to grapple with difficult topics in challenging times (Forstater *et al.* 2006).

So, returning to the climate change example above, is it fair for national government to ask citizens to forgo cheap overseas flights for their holidays when ministers are perceived to ride round in large-engine, chauffeur-driven vehicles and own several homes around the world? Possibly not.

This is where local authorities come back in. Leaders in local government have a critical role to play on the ground in visibly demonstrating first that we are doing our bit. Returning to the climate change example once more, this may, for example, involve making schools and council buildings more energy-efficient or reducing business miles. (Each of these examples is explored with others in greater depth in Part III.)

Just as importantly, it is also about local government putting in place an enabling environment to help the local communities you serve to do their bit, too. It is this concept that we now turn our attention to.

3.3 **Habit-forming behaviour change**

So, assuming we now have a desirable argument for change, how can local authorities best support people to take action?

Revisiting the art of persuasion referred to above, an increasingly popular approach is the use of the '4 Es'—Engage, Emote, Empower, and Enforce—or some variation thereof put forward by many, not least by Caldwell (2008). Put simply, this involves reaching out to inform people (Engage), linking the need to act to an emotional anchor by relating it to close-to-home issues (Emote), before giving people the tools to act (Empower) and eventually, enforcing the behaviour either as it becomes the norm or rather, so it *becomes* the norm (Enforce).

Empowerment can take a number of forms including training and awareness or through the creation of stakeholder groups as we saw earlier with natural resource management in the Philippines. Enforcement, too, can be rolled out in a variety of ways such as changing people's job descriptions as well as issuing public disorder penalties or even removing unhelpful choices in the first place such as energy-inefficient light bulbs.

FIGURE 3.3 **Enabling and sustaining change at the council**

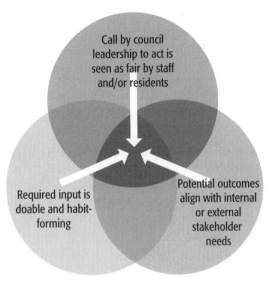

The issue of enforcement is explored in more detail in Part IV; for now, it is important to focus on engaging, emoting, empowering and in particular habit-forming behaviour change. This is depicted in Figure 3.3 where the ideal route to enabling and sustaining change is the centre where the circles intersect.

Walker (2010) refers to the consistency heuristic—that is, a well-researched psychological phenomenon where behaviour leads opinion—'I do it, therefore it makes sense'. In essence, to maintain our beliefs that we are rational and sane we match our behaviours to what we think makes sense and if we change our behaviours then we adapt our relevant opinions to suit. The key thing here is identifying behaviours that chime with people's values or needs and have tangible benefits; we are clear on what we are asking people to do, to create opportunities to catalyse change and then keep reinforcing the sense that it is normal for people to act in this new way.

Then, as 'new' behaviour becomes the 'norm', it becomes 'unchallengeable' as it is aligned to beliefs; it then creates political space for local government to enforce compliance further down the line.

Mandating behaviour change, though, comes with a cautionary note, too: for instance, a body of work by Ostrom (1990) explored how people come together to preserve their collective resources through a purposeful mix of mutually agreed and enforced rules. That is, compliance needs to be handled in an appropriate way. The 2009 Nobel Prize Joint Winner for Economic Governance challenges the assumption that without regulation or the involvement of private enterprise no progress to change individual behaviour can be made. This is explored further below and in Box 3.3.

> ### BOX 3.3 Changing habits through cooperation?
>
> Ostrom cites examples of good practice that benefit all from commonly managed resources: for instance, communal tenure in high mountain meadows in Switzerland. She notes that this 'promotes both general access to and optimum production from certain types of resources while enjoining on the entire community the conservation measures necessary to protect these resources from destruction' (Ostrom 1990).
>
> In contrast, Ostrom also finds that governmentally imposed restrictions are often counterproductive because central authorities lack local knowledge and have insufficient legitimacy.

The balance between voluntary and mandated initiatives brings us neatly to our first case study, from Montgomery County Government.

[#1] Greening operations through behaviour change: Montgomery County, Maryland, USA

Montgomery County is located in the US state of Maryland adjacent to Washington, DC. It boasts a culturally and ethnically diverse population approaching 1 million inhabitants. In 2006, Isiah Leggett became the first African American to be elected Chief Executive. The County benefits from having one of the country's most educated populations in terms of advanced degrees held. Significant employers include the Federal Government, biotechnology companies and small business incubation.

According to Douglas Weisburger, Senior Planning Specialist, Sustainability Programs in the Department for Environmental Protection (DEP), the County Government has enjoyed a number of successes on sustainability matters over the past three years, notably the RainScapes Rewards Program; the establishment of the County's first Climate Protection Plan; and the Green Business Certification Program.

The RainScapes Rewards Program, for instance, is an incentive scheme that has encouraged residents and businesses to install stormwater management controls on their property. Residents and businesses are eligible for up to US$1,200 and US$5,000, respectively, for rebates on rain gardens, conservation landscaping, permeable pavers, trees, rain barrels and green roofs.

Under the new Climate Protection Plan, one of the 58 actions is to replicate the successful establishment of grass-roots environmental organisations through public–private partnerships given their enormous potential to mobilise communities. Bethesda Green is the first such partnership which includes businesses, residents and County legislators among others. It provides a vehicle for promoting existing County programs and is entrepreneurial and nimble, creating environmental education and business development opportunities that the County Government cannot easily or quickly do on its own.

Despite being in the midst of the global credit crisis, with many departments in County Government required to cut their budgets by 25% for the coming year, the DEP has only been marginally affected. This is because the DEP has funding from sources outside of the General Fund (revenue largely from property and income taxes). For example, DEP is funded in large part through the Water Quality Protection Fund and the Solid Waste Fund. In other words it does not have to 'compete' with all other departments for revenue since these are designated for environmental programmes. The RainScapes Rewards Program, for instance, is funded through the Water Quality Protection Fund.

In addition, the DEP is benefiting enormously from the Obama administration's stimulus funding; it has received US$7.6 million in grant funding, which is more than half the total budget not including solid waste. A number of new projects are planned for the coming year using these one-time federal funds.

Building on this successful platform, says Weisburger 'the DEP is now working internally with all county departments to consider an awareness campaign and training program to promote "low hanging fruit", behaviour change actions that either save money or are cost neutral'. Actions currently being considered include:

- Reducing paper use

- Reducing use of bottled water and disposable kitchen-ware

- Increasing the percentage of environmentally responsible products relative to conventional products (e.g. paper, office supplies, furniture, food for office functions, cleaning products, appliances, etc.)

- Increasing recycling rates

- Reducing non-essential electronic equipment and appliances such as fax machines, printers, computers, mini-refrigerators, fans, coffee machines, water coolers, space heaters, etc.

- Increasing the percentage of employees that telecommute and commute to work by public transit, car/vanpool, biking and walking

- Decreasing fleet mileage and idling

- Increasing the use of environmentally friendly technological solutions (e.g. teleconferencing, electronic forms, double-sizing defaults, scanning, printing/copying account codes, power management features, etc.)

- Increasing opportunities for learning about sustainability, with participation by the council's chief executive and president (e.g. courses, training videos, brown bag discussions, signage, etc.)

- Reducing unwanted mail

The hope and intent is that all departments have to be on board and feel empowered. 'This will not be easy, but we have to create a culture in which sustainability is embedded in every day decisions', continues Weisburger.

The vision for greening operations through behaviour change is that the government will lead by example, whereby its departments will ultimately 'compete' to 'out-green' one another and are rewarded and recognised for their environmental achievements.

While the programme is still in its conceptual infancy, it outlines a three-phase implementation approach involving: awareness raising, training and baseline assessments; followed by an inter-department assistance programme and new purchasing guidelines; and then finally a department competition, certification and incentive scheme, with sustainability reporting to capture the outcomes.

For further information visit www.montgomerycountymd.gov (accessed 14 September 2010).

As is evident from Montgomery County's vision here, they want to build on past successes by incentivising staff to engage in positive behaviour, and make it desirable by profiling and rewarding good practice among peers across the council. In addition, to ensure it is habit-forming, they are reporting the outcomes, as well as involving the highest levels of management given the participation in the scheme of the chief executive and president.

This bring us nicely to the next chapter, which focuses on how local government can continue to do much more with a lot less.

Key learning

✓ Making change desirable often means speaking with sceptics, which requires us to make compelling points on relevant issues based on credible peer commentary as well as quality data.

✓ By bridging any perceived gap in fairness, you will go a long way to persuading people of an argument because it is about everyone doing their bit.

✓ Habit-forming behaviour change is a pathway to lasting success and is about engaging, emoting, empowering and enforcing internal and external stakeholders on the big sustainability issues.

Part II

DOING MUCH
MORE WITH A LOT LESS

Route mapping

Part I **The dentist's chair**

Why you should read this book [Chapter 1]	**The big dilemmas faced by local government leaders** [Chapter 2]	**Making change desirable** [Chapter 3]

Part II **Doing much more with a lot less**

The perfect storm [Chapter 4]	**Revisiting the business case** [Chapter 5]	**Criteria for selection of interventions** [Chapter 6]

Part III **The upside of down with amazing people**

Democracy and decision-making [Chapter 7]	**Corporate assets and resources** [Chapter 8]	**Economic development and planning** [Chapter 9]	**Waste and environmental services** [Chapter 10]	**Fleet and logistics** [Chapter 11]	**Community management** [Chapter 12]

Part IV **Out of the darkness: golden rules of excellence in austerity**

Battling back [Chapter 13]	**Reaffirming what is meant by excellence** [Chapter 14]	**Over to you** [Chapter 15]

4

The perfect storm

When a city accepts as its mandate its quality of life; when it respects the people who live in it; when it respects the environment; when it prepares for future generations; the people share responsibility for that mandate, and this shared case is the only way to achieve the collective dream (Jaime Lerner, former Mayor of Curitiba, Brazil, 2009).

Typical sustainability actions and outcomes	Cost-neutral interventions
4.1 Combining bad news	—
4.2 The beginning of the end for the green stimulus?	—
4.3 Seizing the opportunity	—

4.1 **Combining bad news**

The online encyclopaedia Wikipedia defines a 'perfect storm' as 'an event where a rare combination of circumstances aggravate a situation drastically . . . a hypothetical hurricane that happens to hit at a region's most vulnerable area, resulting in the worst possible damage'. This is the fate set to befall local government over at least the next three to five years, as illustrated in Figure 4.1.1.

In short, national targets and public expectations on sustainability matters are increasing at the very same time as funds from national government are being drastically cut.

FIGURE 4.1.1 **Rising obligations with decreasing spending**

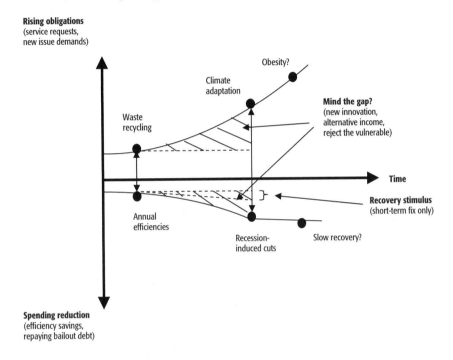

As the world attempts to slowly emerge from the second 'great depression' we have a huge debt burden to service. And, according to O'Hara (2010), taking a historical perspective, while this is not a unique situation in terms of high levels of government borrowing (e.g. Japan and Italy), reductions will not be easily achieved (the mass, violent public protests in Greece during 2010 bear witness to this). One consequence of this is that local government will face frightening budget pressures over the coming years, with emergency spending cuts to reduce the debt burden of anything up to 40% (on top of the usual annual efficiency savings) over the next half decade or so from 2010 onwards; regardless of the political persuasion of the ruling administrations. Yet, at the same time, national sustainability targets are on the increase. To begin to understand why, look at Figure 4.1.2 on world carbon emissions. For example, under the UK Climate Change Act 2007 various actors will be required to reduce emissions by 80% by 2050 which will require significant investment by councils. However, this also coincides with rising public requests for support by local government (for instance local businesses which are teetering on failure, or vulnerable citizens who have lost life savings or employment and who need a lifeline). Add to this other dilemmas such as the pressures on access to clean drinking water, growth in obesity and energy security, then the widening gap between obligations and expenditure appears frightening for local governments who are being tasked to be at the forefront of the battle.

To illustrate the point further, let us look at one of these big challenges in more detail: namely, sustainable consumption.

4.1.1 Economic growth, population and consumption

Similar to interpretations of sustainable development, sustainable consumption can mean different things to different people, too. One definition is that used by the United Nations (UN) whereby sustainable consumption is:

> The use of services and related products which respond to basic needs and bring a better quality of life while minimising the use of natural resources and toxic materials as well as emissions of waste and pollutants over the life cycle of the service or product so as not to jeopardise the needs of future generations (UN Commission on Sustainable Development 1994).

According to the World Business Council for Sustainable Development (WBCSD 2008), global consumption levels and patterns are driven at the most fundamental level by a combination of rapid global population growth, the rise in global affluence among middle- and lower-income consumers, and a culture of 'consumerism' among higher-income groups. That is, global population is projected to rise by about a third to 9 billion by 2050, world gross domestic product (GDP) is expected to grow by 325% during this time and, on average, about 60% of GDP is currently spent on consumer goods. Recent studies such as that by WWF (2006) show humankind are already exceeding the Earth's ability to support many people's comfortable lifestyles and have been doing so for more than 20 years. According to WWF, humankind's 'ecological footprint' (a measure of the pressure on the Earth from human consumption of natural resources) has already increased to 125% of global carrying capacity and could rise to 170% by 2040. To contextualise this, 1 billion people are currently without access to clean drinking water according to the UN (Jowett 2010), which makes the pursuit of the UN's Millennium Development Goals (MDGs) target of halving extreme poverty by 2015 ever more challenging (UN 2009). So, if WBCSD and WWF are correct, humankind either now or in the future is far removed from a 'one planet living' approach—in short, our consumption of the planet's limited natural resources is massively unsustainable and this trend needs to be unreservedly reversed. For some, this means a radical shift in how we use natural resources and for Jackson (2009) this requires a move to 'prosperity without growth' as part of a new economics for a finite planet. Here he stated that economic activities should satisfy three clear principles: a positive contribution to well-being, decent provision of livelihoods and low material and energy use.

Given this baseline for the problem, one can now consider the debate about practical solutions in more depth, specifically a contentious debate on population control versus reduced consumption by affluent individuals.

Two environmental commentators, Jonathon Porritt and George Monbiot, disagree on the solution, although both use carbon emissions as a primary indicator of ecological footprinting. Porritt (2007) advocates population control as a dramatic solution to unsustainable consumption whereas Monbiot (2006) argues that this is unfair and instead affluent individuals should reduce what they consume.

Population control is highly contentious in rich and poor countries alike. Some, such as Porritt, have said the promotion of reproductive education is one of the most progressive forms of intervention. Porritt cites the fact that 'had there been no "one-child family" policy in China there would have been 400 million additional Chinese citizens' and this line of argument is supported by the Optimum Population Trust (Opt). According to them the world's population (presently 6.8 billion) is increasing at nearly 84 million per year and is expected to peak at about 9 billion people in 2050. By this time, the UN Intergovernmental Panel on Climate Change (IPCC 2007) insists global carbon emissions must have been reduced by at least 80% to avoid dangerous rises in temperature, meaning that the carbon footprint of each citizen in 2050 will, therefore, have to reduce to minimal proportions. Furthermore, a cost–benefit analysis by Wire (2009) of the London School of Economics, commissioned by the Opt, claims that family planning is the cheapest way to reduce carbon emissions. Every US$6 spent on contraception, Wire says, saves one tonne of carbon dioxide from contributing to global warming, while a similar reduction in emissions would require a US$12 investment in tree planting, US$22.5 in wind power, US$46.5 in solar energy and US$84 in hybrid vehicle technology. So, Porritt concludes, enhanced family planning is the best available solution to unsustainable consumption.

However, other environmental commentators such as Monbiot refute this and believe that global population is much less important when compared with the effect of increased consumption from economic growth. Monbiot argues that:

> humankind should not anticipate a positive consumption transition from radical family planning. People might populate less as they become richer, but they do not consume less; rather, they consume more. That is, as the habits of the super-rich show, there are no limits to human extravagance.

Here, consumption can be expected to rise with economic growth until the biosphere is irreversibly damaged. Worse still for Monbiot, population control represents the worst kind of paternalism, in that it blames the poor for the excesses of the rich. A paper by Satterthwaite (2009) published in the journal *Environment & Urbanization* appears to support Monbiot's line of argument by demonstrating that the places where the population has been growing fastest are those in which carbon dioxide has been growing most slowly, and vice versa. For example, between 1980 and 2005, sub-Saharan Africa produced 18.5% of the world's population growth and just 2.4% of the growth in carbon dioxide. North America produced 4% of the world's population growth, but 14% of the growth in carbon dioxide; 63% of the world's population growth happened in places with very low emissions. Furthermore, Satterthwaite also points out that around one-sixth of the world's population is so poor that it produces no significant emissions at all, yet this is also the group whose growth rate is likely to be highest. For example, lower-income households in India use a fifth of the electricity per head and one-seventh of the transport fuel of higher-income households in India. Satterthwaite goes on to suggest that the old formula of development, that total impact (I) equals population (P) times affluence (A) times technology (T), $I = P \times A \times T$, is flawed. Instead Satterthwaite argues that total impact should be measured as $I = C \times A \times T$, consumers (C) times affluence (A) times technology (T). Many of the world's people use so little technology that they would not figure in this equation, yet they are the ones who have most children. Thus Monbiot concludes 'While there is a weak correlation between global warming and population growth, there is a strong correlation between global warming and wealth'.

What appears to be clear is that, in terms of economic growth, the point of departure for both is broadly the same. That is, for Porritt and Monbiot, economic growth is incompatible with sustainable development and, so, sustainable consumption is important. An apparent strength of Porritt's call for greater population control is that it provides a favourable cost–benefit for family planning versus other carbon-reducing investments such as tree planting or solar power. On the downside, this could be perceived as prejudicing the economically powerful over the economically weak. By comparison, Monbiot's strength is the evidence base to support the targeting of individual affluent consumers who would seem to have a much greater propensity to consume, whether in the developed or developing world. A potential weakness in Monbiot's case, however, is that, given the world's population is expected to increase dramatically, and that we have already gone way beyond the Earth's carrying capacity, reining in individual consumption among the affluent may be difficult to do without precedent. Unlike, for example, China's one-child family policy. That is, it lacks the legitimacy of having been mandated somewhere in the world already.

Our dependence on fossil fuels has led to excess amounts of greenhouse gases such as CO_2 being pumped into the atmosphere, which traps heat and has resulted in the warming of our planet; bad news for everyone, especially for those in poverty. As Figure 4.1.2 shows, carbon emissions vary per capita and per country. While China as a

FIGURE 4.1.2 **World carbon emissions**

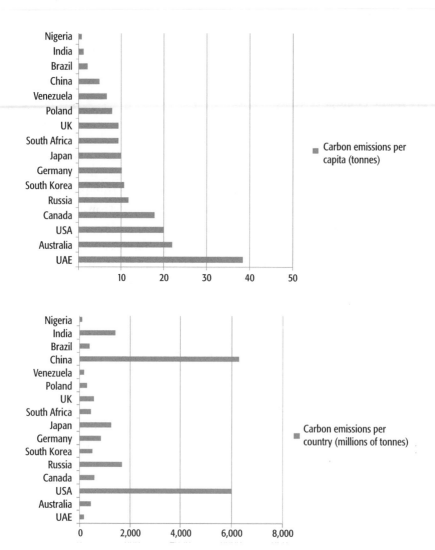

whole produces more emissions than the USA, emissions arising from each of China's citizens are just one-fifth of those of the USA. This raises challenges in terms of sustainable consumption and fairness. If China continues to grow apace then high standards of living will lead to more consumption and, thus, more emissions. But is it fair for US citizens to expect Chinese citizens not to aspire to their standard of living? If not, perhaps a desirable outcome for all is prosperity that does not kill the planet?

So, what does this mean for local governments which have an intervention role in family planning? Well, while both arguments have their merits in terms of a compelling scientific evidence base, there may be limitations to any single, capture-all solution. Indeed, a hybrid model may be preferable, for instance by a voluntary opt-in or opt-out model, drawing on Ostrom's work referred to above. (This idea is explored further in Chapter 12.)

Returning to our broader perfect storm scenario, as noted earlier, the role of the 'green stimulus' is important here, but just how important?

4.2 **The beginning of the end for the green stimulus?**

Despite the enormous sums of money forthcoming under the green stimulus spending referred to in Chapter 2, the World Research Institute (WRI) has cautioned us to keep this in perspective. It argues that even the most aggressive short-term stimulus spending will have only a modest impact on emissions and that recovery efforts should be designed to set the stage for more comprehensive sustainability policies (Bendell and Cohen 2009).

Brown (2009), in his Plan B budget, attempts to calculate the cost of this transformational change and concludes that the additional annual expenditure to meet social and environmental goals is US$187 billion, as summarised in Table 4.2.

TABLE 4.2 **The cost of saving the planet?**

Goal	Funding (US$ billions)
BASIC SOCIAL GOALS	
Universal primary education	10
Eradication of adult illiteracy	4
School lunch programmes for 44 poor countries	6
Assistance to pre-school children and pregnant women in 44 poor countries	4
Reproductive health and family planning	17
Universal basic healthcare	33
Closing the condom gap	3
Sub-total	77
EARTH RESTORATION GOALS	
Planting trees to reduce flooding and conserve soil	6
Planting trees to sequester carbon	17
Protecting topsoil on cropland	24
Restoring rangelands	9
Restoring fisheries	13
Protecting biological diversity	31
Stabilising water tables	10
Sub-total	110
GRAND TOTAL	187

Source: Brown 2009

Based on data from the UN World Food Programme, Brown claims the cost of saving the planet is equivalent to just 13% of the global military budget and so goes on to argue that money will be better spent by diverting resources to avoiding conflict arising from environmental deterioration, poverty and population growth.

So, in effect, an annual long-term green stimulus is being put forward here. However, it does not require additional money, just a diversion of some of the existing money already being spent. 'All the problems we face can be dealt with using existing technologies. And almost everything we need to do to move the world economy back onto an environmentally sustainable path has already been done in one or more countries' (Brown 2009).

In addition to redirecting spending, though, one can also consider ways to reduce needless and environmentally harmful subsidies. For instance, since 1994, the Green Scissors Campaign, led by Friends of the Earth, Taxpayers for Common Sense and US Public Interest Research Group, has been working with the US Congress and the Administration to end environmentally harmful and unnecessary spending. Working to breach party lines, the Green Scissors Campaign has helped cut more than US$26 billion in environmentally wasteful programmes from the federal budget (Green Scissors 2010).

In the main, however, these calls would appear to have fallen on deaf ears for the time being (albeit with some notable exceptions, such as South Korea's low-carbon investment). So where does this leave a local council that is not benefiting from short-term or long-term green stimulus packages and is not able to identify perverse subsidies to abolish?

4.3 Seizing the opportunity

Paradoxically, the financial crisis represents a unique opportunity for leaders in local government to take more radical, 'game-changing' positive action.

To bridge the gap between spending limits and service obligations, councils will either have to: make further dramatic efficiency savings, reduce services on offer, identify new income streams or realise novel product or process innovations. This will create new political space for leaders to consider transformational change.

History teaches us that this is possible, too. Following his State of the Union address in 1942 after the bombing of Pearl Harbour, President Roosevelt banned the automobile industry from making cars for three years so they could switch to manufacturing 45,000 tanks, 60,000 planes, 20,000 anti-aircraft guns and several thousand ships. The mobilisation of enormous resources within a matter of months demonstrates that a country and, indeed, the world can restructure the economy quickly if convinced of the need to do so (Brown 2009). And Roosevelt's words in 1942 are as relevant today—'Let no man say it cannot be done'.

Which brings us back to desirability.

We can, and should, take urgent action now to move towards a sustainable way of living. Regardless of whether Brown's Plan B budget materialises, we all need to do what we can. This is especially true for local government leaders, given the pivotal role you play in serving our communities.

As detailed in this book, there are a vast number of 'habit-forming' actions on sustainability that leaders in local government can take which are both high-impact, and most crucially in the current financial climate, cost-neutral to do and this is as true for Mumbai and Johannesburg as it is for Krakow or New York.

We turn to this in the next section, but first we need to make sure our respective business case is robust.

Key learning

✓ Councils are operating a perfect storm of reduced spending, higher public service needs and increased sustainability targets.

✓ Short-term green stimuli are helpful, but will not be sufficient in the long term to bridge the shortfall.

✓ The financial crisis presents an opportunity for council leaders to advance game-changing activities and the cost-neutral interventions proposed here will be helpful to you in making this happen.

5
Revisiting the business case

Cities really can be another actor that can pressure and open doors for new negotiations . . . This is a serious issue, climate change, so we cannot leave this issue to governments only (Marcelo Ebrard, Mayor of Mexico City 2009).

Typical sustainability actions and outcomes	Cost-neutral interventions
5.1 Context is all important	–
5.2 Things to consider when refining or rebuilding	#2

5.1 **Context is all-important**

In re-examining your business case to take action on sustainability issues it is critical to understand how this is constantly shaped by your particular context. As we saw in the previous section, defining, or indeed redefining, what is most important or material to us changes from context to context (Zadek and Merme 2003) and is informed by a number of factors such as strategic goals, available resources, local culture, national law or shifts over time.

Building on the sentiments of Mayor Ebrard, above, another great example of this in the public sector is the USA's department for defence (Goldenberg 2010): 'The department takes climate change very seriously', according to Amanda Dory, Deputy Assistant Secretary of US Defence for Strategy 2010, after announcing the Pentagon will produce 25% of its electricity from renewables.

So, why is the Pentagon (which accounts for 80% of US government energy consumption) so worried about climate change? Is it concerned about its cost of operations? Or, maybe it's emissions? Or is it more to do with energy security? The above quote by Dory followed closely after a public study by the Head of the US Army stating that 'peak oil'—the point at which the demand and ability to pay for oil exceeds its available supply—will be reached in 2015. The result of this will not only be barriers to development in the developed and developing world and new forms of conflict over natural resources, but also a heightened risk for the US to maintain its defences because of its over-reliance on a fuel produced overseas. In short, the business case for the US Secretary of Defense to act on climate change is very clear and very strong. Would this have been the case even just a few years earlier? Possibly not, which illustrates how context can shift over time and dramatically affect the business case to act.

The lesson here for us all, including local councils, is that we need to continually review and refresh our business case. It is the foundation of our mandate to act and it is the cornerstone of our ability to persuade others to act, particularly on sustainability matters in these austere times.

So what things do you need to consider when refining or rebuilding your business case?

5.2 Things to consider when refining or rebuilding

As a minimum, a standard checklist for a council working on sustainability matters inspired by Weiser and Zadek (2000) and Forum for the Future (2010) should be as follows:

- Saving money through reduced use of energy and other resources and the avoidance of penalties for waste or polluting

- Compliance with environmental or social legislation relating to pollution controls or diversity

- Better management of risk

- Cultivation of brand, e.g. as an ideal location to invest, work, live and play

- Helping to deliver expected services, e.g. parks or recycling

- Supporting joint investment or implementation with partners who share the council's values or goals, e.g. retraining of the local workforce to fill new low-carbon technology posts or community cohesion to tackle extremism or xenophobia

The case studies, anecdotes and management tips in Part III will assist practitioners in populating the answers to these questions and more.

Just as crucial, however, is that the business case for sustainability is aligned to, and is an integral and demonstrable part of, the core strategy of the council. Indicators and targets of performance should support, inform and shape an authority's key objectives as this way the business case is more likely to gain the political support it deserves. Remember, as we saw in Chapter 3, success of sustainability in these times all comes down to desirability. Think of the University of East Anglia example earlier: sometimes lots of data is not enough and can in fact be counterproductive. And so during a time of unprecedented spending cuts, the value of sustainability to save money for a local council is ever more compelling. We can bring all this together here in Figure 5.2, which brings us to the next case study, an example of resilience planning during pressing times of energy consumption reduction.

FIGURE 5.2 **Managing the business case for sustainability**

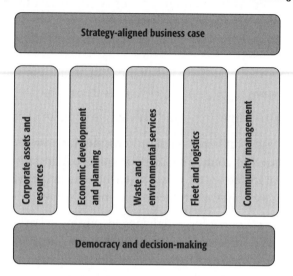

High-impact • Low-cost • Fair • Possible • Desirable • Habit-forming

Strategy-aligned business case

Corporate assets and resources

Economic development and planning

Waste and environmental services

Fleet and logistics

Community management

Democracy and decision-making

Persuasive evidence of need • Credible peer commentators • Quality data

---

[#2] Cutting work hours and consumption in an energy crisis: Caracas Metropolitan Area, Venezuela

Caracas is Venezuela's capital and largest city with a population of over 4 million inhabitants. Caracas comprises five municipalities: the City itself and four that form part of the Metropolitan Area District Council, or Alcaldía del Distrito Metropolitano—Alcaldía de Chacao, Alcaldía de Baruta, Alcaldía El Hatillo and Alcaldía de Sucre. The economy is primarily made up of service, banking and petroleum companies. The city is also seen as the country's cultural centre and is home for a diverse mix of ethnic groups from Europe and Latin America. With all these opportunities, health, poverty and crime remain constant and serious challenges.

While there are explicit environmental protection plans in place for these councils, broader sustainability matters are lower down the priority list, with sustainability budgets very constrained and only accounting for approximately 0.5 to 2.0% of total budgets across the district.

'The focus is on the provision of basic environmental services in relation to waste collection and treatment, public health, and education programmes for children, the youth and senior people', says Lino Clemente, a sustainability adviser.

There are some notable exceptions to this: namely, the success of urban vegetable gardens; and, more pressingly, energy use resilience planning in order to be able to continue to provide the basic environmental services.

In 2009 a government-sponsored, FAO-assisted project created 8,000 micro-gardens of 1 square metre each in the city's barrios, many of them within a few steps of family kitchens. As soon as one crop is mature, it is harvested and immediately replaced with new seedlings. Each square metre, continuously cropped, can produce 330 heads of lettuce, 18 kg of tomatoes, or 16 kg of cabbage per year. The wider goal is to have 100,000 micro-gardens in the country's urban areas and 1,000 hectares of urban compost-based gardens nationwide.

Since 2010 Venezuela has been in the midst of an electricity rationing programme caused, according to the government, by acute water shortages at the main hydroelectric Guri dam, which provides 70% of domestic electricity consumption. The ensuing power cuts have caused chaos with traffic lights and office building use, affecting major energy users such as businesses and the universities in particular. The councils have no control over utility infrastructure planning. And so in an effort to reduce the consumption demand and operating costs from public buildings, a key part of the council's resilience planning has been reducing the working day for state employees to half of normal hours.

The deep crisis will be difficult to resolve because of the dependence on weather improvements, and a lag time of several years in any new government policy in respect of significant utility infrastructure investments. Controversially, President Chávez went on state television admitting that technical errors and poor decisions had been the cause and that as a result he had sacked the country's Electricity Minister, Alì Rodriguez.

The problem is being further exacerbated by the ensuing water shortages.

Going forward for the councils, an increasing emphasis will be placed on institutional capacity building and on establishing new partnerships with community and business groups to help deliver priority environmental and education programmes and continue to alleviate the energy and water emergencies.

For further information visit:

- alcaldiametropolitana.gob.ve/portal
- www.chacao.gov.ve/ipca/ipcadetail.asp?Id=60
- www.contraloriasucre.gob.ve/Imapsas.html
- www.alcaldiaelhatillo.gob.ve
- www.alcaldiadebaruta.gob.ve

(all websites accessed 15 September 2010).

What is particularly insightful about how the Caracas District Councils are working in this particular issue is that, despite national planning policies being outside of their control, and the day-to-day challenges raised by the considerable poverty among their residents, they are working hard to maintain a basic level of essential services such as waste collection and community education by moderating their own energy use. That is, immediately recognising that their business case has changed in a crisis, the councils have reprioritised rapidly and have done so simultaneously reducing operating costs which could then be reinvested in meagre environmental budgets.

Key learning

✓ When revisiting your business case, context is all-important: strategic goals, national law, local culture and available resources.

✓ As part of refining or rebuilding your approach in the current austere climate, think about key drivers that will chime with your council leaders and the public, such as financial savings from resource efficiency.

✓ The key is doing the best you can in your particular circumstances.

6

Criteria for selection of interventions

Why are the public spaces for cars deemed more important than public spaces for children? High quality public pedestrian space in general and parks in particular are evidence of a true democracy at work because they are the only places where people meet as equals (Enrique Peñalosa, former Mayor of Bogotà, Colombia, 2009).

Typical sustainability actions and outcomes	Cost-neutral interventions
6.1 Intervention filtering	–
6.2 Ideas that failed the test	–

6.1 **Intervention filtering**

Before intervening you will need to draw up an interventions list. So, it is important to be clear what constitutes a helpful intervention.

Bringing all the learning together from the earlier chapters allows us to develop a filter to select useful interventions. Essentially this is a matrix, which plots desirable change on the vertical axis against zero cost options on the horizontal axis. The most promising interventions will be in the top right-hand corner quadrant (high desirability and low cost) and the least helpful interventions will be in the bottom left-hand corner quadrant (low desirability and relatively high cost). This is depicted in Figure 6.1 using the examples of thermostat control and smarter driving.

FIGURE 6.1 **Intervention matrix**

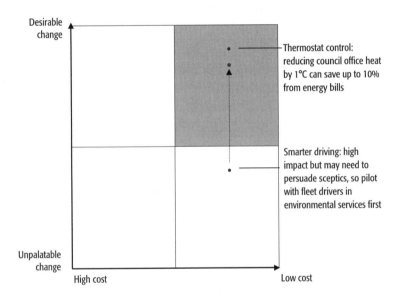

So, to recap, the criteria for your intervention selection is as follows:

- Step 1. Draw up a long list of passive interventions that relate to the issues detailed in Section 2.3 on defining sustainability

- Step 2. Select from this list those that would be considered desirable and indeed habit-forming according to Section 3.3

- Step 3. Run a final filter according to those that are cost-neutral, to derive a final shortlist of 100 interventions

By cost-neutral, here, we mean actions that either involve no additional financial outlay, or where any financial outlay is a net cost, as the investment is returned within a short payback period of five years or less, noting that money will be scarce during the credit crisis. The price of taking action is no more than existing staff time, which may require reprioritising tasks, just as is undertaken in any normal business planning process. Categories of interventions may range from policy development or a procurement shift to behaviour change.

Of course, depending on your business case, which is context-specific, what is desirable for you will differ from council to council; from context to context.

It may be a useful exercise to use the above tool in discussions with your colleagues about the appropriate actions proposed in this book, and could be particularly useful for starting a meaningful dialogue with the sceptics we 'met' in Chapter 3.

6.2 Ideas that failed the test

We can learn a lot from what did not 'make the grade'.

To give you a flavour of what definitely qualifies, what may or may not qualify but can be leveraged up, and what definitely does not qualify refer again to Figure 6.1.

Turning down the thermostat to save on unnecessary energy consumption is a free and easy way to save money. Smarter driving can be free, too, or possibly involve some minor upfront costs which will be repaid from fuel savings later on; perhaps piloting it first in one willing part of the business, such as the waste collection fleet that resides in environmental services, would make it a better selection. (See Chapters 8 and 11, respectively, for more details on each.)

By comparison, some possible interventions did not make the grade, because they failed to meet one or more of the criteria. This does not mean such interventions are not helpful, but simply that they are beyond the scope of qualifying interventions. Examples include:

- Large-scale renewable energy or transport fuel investments, owing to the scale of cost and lengthy payback period. Although councils can still have a massive impact on this through planning (see Chapter 9 for more details)

- Asking people not to fly. This fails simply on desirability grounds as there is an absence of fairness in many people's eyes between their overseas holiday and council leaders riding around in enormous cars. An alternative tactic is asking people to support the domestic tourist industry (something we return to in Chapter 12)

- Registering as a carbon offset project, a mechanism by which one organisation pays another organisation to compensate for its inability to sufficiently reduce its carbon footprint (for instance, through the planting of new trees that would not otherwise be grown). This is deemed beyond the scope of this book as councils have a duty to *reduce* emissions and so would not adhere to the strict 'additionality' rule for offsetting, even if, say, a council wanted to use it to fund important initiatives such as green spaces. The additionality rule requires an action to be on top of what should already be happening; that is, without intervention, it would not otherwise occur

Of course, some of these omissions may be open to dispute, depending on your particular context. By debating these with your colleagues it will make your selection process even more robust and defensible to the external world!

All of which bring us to the next section of this book. In Part III we move to the next level of detail in terms of how each function of a council can practically implement cost-neutral and powerful sustainability initiatives. In essence, this part is the main source of the numerous tips and anecdotes contained in this book. We begin, naturally, with 'Democracy and decision-making'. Why? Because it is from this that all other changes can be directed by leaders.

Key learning

✓ It is important for you to be clear on what is and what is not a smart intervention on sustainability matters and why this is the case.

✓ Desirable, cost-neutral interventions are particularly helpful to the delivery of your business goals in austere times.

Part III

THE UPSIDE OF DOWN WITH AMAZING PEOPLE

Route mapping

Part I   **The dentist's chair**

Why you should read this book [Chapter 1]	**The big dilemmas faced by local government leaders** [Chapter 2]	**Making change desirable** [Chapter 3]

Part II   **Doing much more with a lot less**

The perfect storm [Chapter 4]	**Revisiting the business case** [Chapter 5]	**Criteria for selection of interventions** [Chapter 6]

Part III   **The upside of down with amazing people**

Democracy and decision-making [Chapter 7]	**Corporate assets and resources** [Chapter 8]	**Economic development and planning** [Chapter 9]	**Waste and environmental services** [Chapter 10]	**Fleet and logistics** [Chapter 11]	**Community management** [Chapter 12]

Part IV   **Out of the darkness: golden rules of excellence in austerity**

Battling back [Chapter 13]	**Reaffirming what is meant by excellence** [Chapter 14]	**Over to you** [Chapter 15]

7

Democracy and decision-making

Democracy doesn't recognise east or west; democracy is simply people's will. Therefore, I do not acknowledge that there are various models of democracy; there is just democracy itself (Shirin Ebadi, Nobel Peace Prize Winner, Iran, 2003).

Typical sustainability actions and outcomes	Cost-neutral interventions
7.1 Recalibrating the rules	#48, #11
7.2 Being able to take the right decision	#49, #50, #12, #3
7.3 Warts-and-all communications	#51, #13, #52
7.4 The next generation	#14

7.1 **Recalibrating the rules**

Often, local government is, by its very nature, a delegation of powers and duties from national government that govern how a council serves its communities. The 'rulebook' for how this is organised is usually captured in a formal document sometimes called a constitution. Primary among these rules are how members of the public are elected to office to serve, the public standards they must observe as councillors, how these councillors then work with the paid council officers to make decisions, and the key issues or decisions that must be managed (including sustainability matters i.e. compliance with national targets for carbon emissions as well as other environmental laws).

So in essence councils are mini-democratic states that enable local citizens to pursue our freedoms. And, as Grayling (2007) reminds us, this system did not evolve easily—with 'people struggled and died for it' in the recounting of the story of the struggles for liberty and rights. Therefore, as democracy is so crucial it is *vital* that such rule-making is calibrated in the right way, and this provides us with a powerful platform here to explore a number of these issues in more detail from a sustainability viewpoint. To do this we must get our sequence of interventions (as illustrated in Fig. 7.1) right, and so each aspect is now explored.

FIGURE 7.1 **Sequencing actions on democracy and decision-making**

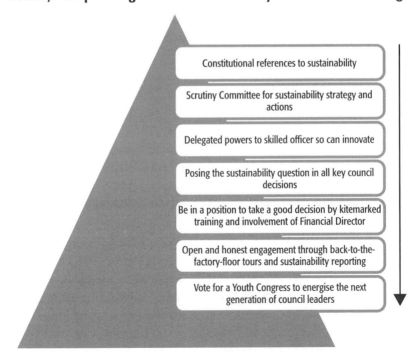

First, with regard to accountability, one suggestion is the establishment of a sustainability scrutiny committee(s). As the name suggests, the role here is to scrutinise sustainability strategies and action plans to ensure they remain aligned to core corporate objectives and to debate contentious or sometimes conflicting dilemmas in addition to regularly monitoring project performance. This is both a powerful platform to hold officers to account and a fantastic way to showcase good work and maintain political champions for one's efforts. Yet, although this has high strategic and political gains, it costs no more than officer and member time.

[#48] **Who watches the watchers? Committee for scrutiny committees**

At the risk of becoming over-bureaucratic, it can often be sound practice to establish a committee of councillors who will oversee a council's suite of scrutiny committees. This provides strong oversight by coordinating the schemes to be scrutinised and forward planning accordingly; such a committee ensures there is joined-up thinking on cross-cutting sustainability matters.

In terms of the delegation of powers, it is imperative that there is scope to innovate between councillors and council officers, as shown by Malmö Council in Sweden (Forum for the Future 2010). However, while very useful, this should, critically, work in conjunction with a robust scrutinising process as detailed above.

[#11] **Permission to show creativity in Malmö, Sweden**

Within Malmö Council, employees at officer level are given the opportunity and the permission to show creativity in addressing sustainability problems to improve their areas. While the political leadership retains an overarching view, it allows those with on-the-ground experience and knowledge to find appropriate solutions.

One way your council could do this would be to let officers determine how a particular type of waste, such as food from domestic kitchens, should be collected once leadership has mandated it must happen: for example, in terms of the frequency of food collection, proposed re-use and so on.

In addition, as well as business-as-usual sustainability matters, emerging problems may require 'new' solutions and approaches that may be unusual. For example it may be necessary to forge new partnerships between the public, private and non-profit sectors, and could take the form of area- or issue-based stakeholder groups (e.g. looking at green spaces, crime or employment). This could require a novel approach to working and a shift in culture, as well as delegated powers in some instances.

But how should considerations of sustainability matters in all decision-making take place? As with most large and professional organisations, councils often have generic templates or documents for officers to prepare papers for leadership to base key decisions on. We explore this further now in the next tip.

[#49] Posing the sustainability question

Key decision papers often have standard headings such as purpose, recommendations and background, as well as a number of impact assessments related to risk, finance, personnel, IT and human resources. Depending on national law, some may also have specific equality of opportunity or diversity assessments for the wider community (for instance, the black economic empowerment law in South Africa). However, there is clearly a need for sustainability matters to be included too!

There is an opportunity to include specific environmental sustainability assessments, notably carbon footprint or the use of natural resources, and may cover, among other things, decision-making on new construction or building refurbishment, substantial travel or major procurement. Attached to each of these points should be guidelines and a checklist so that non-environmental managers are able to self-assess or know where to seek help from technical experts. The checklist of impacts to be considered should include as a minimum: energy use, waste creation, water use or pollution arising. This checklist would then require the officer to propose a justification for the decision, with suggested improvements or mitigation controls against these impacts.

Awareness raising and communications in line with this should be delivered prior to introduction (e.g. to be included in senior manager inductions). Then following its introduction, a review of papers and key decisions should be undertaken to determine the quality of responses the process has generated.

So, as we have seen here, the right balance between scrutiny and delegation as well as how key decisions are presented to leadership is core to success.

7.2 **Being able to take the right decision**

Having the 'rules' in place to *make* effective decisions is necessary, but unfortunately not sufficient on its own to be able to *take* the right decisions. This requires having the appropriate individual and organisational competences too. There a number of ways one can approach this in local government, and we begin with a suggestion on training.

[#50] Towards a Kitemark for leadership

As a minimum, the induction package for all new officers and elected members should include details of the council's sustainability work. This includes any corporate environmental policies and risk-related issues.

But more than this, the leadership team's continuing professional development would be enhanced by formal reviews and assessments on sustainability matters. For instance, senior managers in local government are often required to undergo in-house or external training that is accredited to a certain standard in public sector management. A module devoted entirely to sustainability issues would provide a Kitemark to certify the leaders of tomorrow.

Taking this a step further would mean senior managers or elected members would not be promoted to higher office unless they had successfully completed this course, as an indicator of competence.

The power of this is that it would tease out, and legitimise, sustainability champions at all levels of leadership, and across all issues—whether it be climate change or equal opportunities.

There are other ways to look at this, of course. Take, for instance, the separate but related approaches by the Greater London Authority and Woking Council in the UK (Forum for the Future 2010). This is illustrated by the following anecdote.

[#12] **Making sure the right people are in the room in London and Woking, UK**

Having the right people in the room together has proved to be of immense benefit for local government leaders in the UK.

The Greater London Authority (GLA) is a big advocate of having a clear link between those that are writing sustainability strategies and those that are responsible for their delivery. The GLA's Climate Change Agency and Transport for London both have delegated responsibility for developing and delivering their own action plans.

By comparison, Woking Council has often listed the involvement of the finance director in key decisions on sustainability matters as an enabler for sustainability. This ensures that a solid business case for practical action to take place is robust in financial terms, such as costs that can be avoided by using resources more efficiently.

Again the cost of investment here of making things happen is just your people's time and effort. But what wider protocols of environmental-related decision-making are helpful to councils? And how do these work in practice? Possible answers to these questions set us up for the next in-depth case study which considers the impacts of environmental decision-making and leadership.

[#3] **Environmental decision-making and leadership: City of Ekurhuleni, South Africa**

Ekurhuleni Metropolitan Municipality forms the local government of the East Rand region of Gauteng, South Africa (the name *Ekurhuleni* means place of peace in Xitsonga). Ekurhuleni is one of the six districts of Gauteng province of South Africa and one of the six metropolitan municipalities of South Africa with a population of nearly 2.5 million, three-quarters of whom are black Africans.

While the area was historically one of the largest producers of gold, the major economic sectors now include manufacturing, wholesale and trade, energy and financial services. Despite having a high proportion of people of working age, the unemployment rate is high at about 40%. Approximately one-fifth of people reside in informal or inadequate housing.

The Municipality states that it is committed to sound environmental management principles as evidenced by the development of its Environmental Management Framework (EMF) (the first municipality to do so in the country); State of the Environment (SoE) reports; a new biodiversity and open space strategy; and successfully hosting a youth and environment conference and winter camp, focusing on climate change and natural resources management.

A key challenge remains ensuring the fair distribution of the economic benefits of its new and heritage industries while managing the environmental impacts associated with these activities. According to Kobedi Pilane, the council's environmental protection practitioner:

> It helps to a have a vision and some understanding of the concepts of environmental management among officials and the political leadership. The community is not stupid, they read and some are well informed so would be well placed to expose the council for wasting resources with uninformed projects.

The purpose of the EMF is to provide leadership with a decision support system that will help the authority to execute its respective mandates in a coordinated, objective and efficient manner. It is important to note that the EMF will not be a 'blueprint' land-use plan for the area but a decision support mechanism that takes environmental as well as socioeconomic factors into account for each individual decision that has to be made.

The purpose of SoE reporting is to provide information on the condition of the environment to various stakeholders in the public and private sectors, in order for them to deal with and understand environmental problems. The provision of this information is intended to set the basis for the development of policy and strategies, allow the monitoring of progress and performance of implemented policy and programmes, and raise public awareness of environmental issues. More specifically, the objectives are to:

- Collate available baseline information and data

- Identify gaps in knowledge and data and through the identification of issues, make recommendations for closing the gaps

- Present baseline descriptions of the following: the human environment; cultural heritage resources; land use and capability, soils and agricultural potential and geology; water resources; the atmosphere; ecosystems and biodiversity; pollution and waste; and environmental management and governance; make recommendations for the indicators for future use; and identify strategic priorities to be addressed in policy development

Emphasising that the council is constantly challenged in terms of available resources and the ongoing need to build in-house awareness and capacity at the highest levels, Pilane adds:

> What we can do is to seek partnerships with relevant NGOs and raise community awareness on smart living for a greener future. We cannot encourage positive behaviour without environmental strategies that will develop environmental education and awareness to ensure that we have an informed citizenry.

For further information visit www.ekurhuleni.com (accessed 15 September 2010).

So again, similar to Caracas, Ekurhuleni shows us that significant in-house, low-cost efforts can advance sustainability practices through intelligence and commitment.

7.3 **Warts-and-all communications**

As hard as this is for you to do, transparent communications on both good results and the areas for improvement is invaluable in retaining credibility and trust for driving performance improvements (Rubbens *et al.* 2002). And although communications has traditionally been seen as just reporting, for you to achieve trustworthy and valuable communications the importance of cascading messages from leaders to the lowest levels of the organisation and vice versa should not be underestimated. Going back to the 'factory floor' can take a number of forms.

[#51] **Back to the factory floor**

Senior managers should take the opportunity at least once a year, to spend 'a day in the life' of a member of their workforce. Whether it is emptying refuse bins or mowing the grass in parks, any leader will gain valuable insight from the experience: in terms of learning about the areas of strength or weakness in particular policies or procedures or through bonding with colleagues.

Other ways to engage might be annual staff conferences where key messages are shared, in terms of successes to celebrate and failings to learn from, and this can be an ideal platform for people at all levels of the organisation to be heard and recognised.

Similarly, with elected members, so-called 'seeing is believing' or 'walking and talking' tours with residents in particularly hard-hit areas provide hands-on learning about what does and does not work on the ground.

Of course, one main way of demonstrating a warts-and-all approach is via public reporting. However, as local government is often already under statutory requirements to report on various sustainability matters ranging from pollution control to disability, there is often perceived to be little motivation for doing more. As shown by Rubbens *et al.* (2002), the value of voluntarily disclosing your performance, risks and opportunities to a particular target audience is large; and as relevant to internal as it is to external stakeholders. This tip is supported by the experiences of councils in Australia in particular, as we see next.

> [#13] **Impacts of reporting in Melbourne and Brisbane, Australia**
>
> The City of Melbourne and Brisbane City Council have made significant attempts to integrate planning and reporting using the Global Reporting Initiative (GRI). The UN-sponsored GRI is a reporting framework for disclosing triple-bottom-line performance on issues ranging from job creation and human rights to pollution control and sustainable procurement.
>
> The GRI has been developed in partnership with businesses, governments, trade unions, investors and civil society organisations. The intended benefit of using the GRI is that it allows for benchmarking across a particular sector so that report users can compare and contrast their own performance better.
>
> For a local council, using an externally benchmarked reporting framework builds legitimacy and allows people to take informed decisions: whether they are a prospective employee comparing responsible employers, a resident scrutinising value for money or a company considering various locations for an inward investment opportunity.

This 'impacts of reporting' theory is also depicted in Figure 7.3 and the need for solid reporting is then expanded into two-way reporting after that.

FIGURE 7.3 **Impacts of reporting**

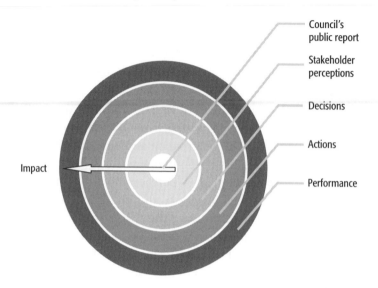

Council's
public report

Stakeholder
perceptions

Decisions

Actions

Impact

Performance

Source: Based on Rubbens *et al.* 2002

[#52] **Letters of support as well as complaint**

Complaints from members of the public are an effective additional
form of holding local government to account for the communities you serve. There are usually clear protocols for handling such
matters, which stem from the constitution as referred to above.
And although they can have a tremendous impact on council officers, just as they would on any professional, it is easy to see how
important they are for a healthy democracy.

However, as officers or elected members, one has a duty to also
suggest to the residents that support for sustainability initiatives
are put in writing, too. Perhaps too often we spend time analysing
dissatisfaction as opposed to satisfaction. This is not about van-
ity accounting, but rather giving power to the council's leadership
for progressive or radical policy initiatives. This can embolden all
to 'compete' for internal resources, particularly during a time of
austerity.

Did you know?

Young people may be disillusioned with politicians but are still passionate about politics, with many participating in youth congresses whereby they get an opportunity to debate the big issues with their peers.

Source: © Catherine Monaghan 2010

However, this is not about lobbying! It is about balance. It is about painting an accurate picture of events, the good as well as the not so good. This is also important for democracy, so it is not just a minority of (affluent or educated) people who know how to complain well and shout loudest that are heard, but also the quietly satisfied majority.

As citizens, we all have a duty to vote, and as Grayling (2007) reminded us, people fought and died for our liberties. Members of the public writing to their elected member to thank them for good public service on a sustainability matter is a powerful statement of intent. We need to embrace it more.

7.4 **The next generation**

When all is said and done, ensuring we have a future generation of leaders is fundamental to successful long-term planning. Not as some benign form of business continuity but to retain the very vitality of politics itself. One novel way of doing this with children and young people is to set up a 'youth congress'. This idea is explored further now.

[#14] **Voting for a youth congress in Oslo, Norway**

School or college elections are not new. However, using this plat-form to re-enact how one's locally elected council operates pro-vides an energising insight into the role and importance of local politics and indeed democracies.

An excellent example of this in action is from Oslo City Council (European Commission 2010), where meetings are chaired and run by young delegates, and they determine which topics and issues are discussed. The young people are invited to consider five pri-ority issues which are being referred for resolution by the city council in ordinary session. Through direct dialogue, the young representatives then discuss proposals with the council's mem-bers.

The added value of such 'theatre' is that it demystifies confus-ing and possibly intimidating machinations of government. In

addition it gives young people the opportunity to practise public speaking and debate at a very tender age, thus building confidence and possibly aspiration.

The model can easily be adapted to different contexts and communities, as it is free and easy to organise. An important intervention could be running this in more areas of the council where
young people badly need valuable role models and a sense of
themselves as active citizens.

Having looked at how the council can take decisions on sustainability, in the next chapter we turn to how we can best utilise the corporate resources at our disposal.

Key learning

✓ Rules of democratic decision-making in councils should
include clear references to sustainability—from the written
constitution to reporting requirements.

✓ Informed decisions on sustainability often require having the
right people involved with the right competences.

✓ A warts-and-all approach to your communications on sustainability is a vital tool to building trust and improving performance.

✓ Encouraging the general public to support good work, recognising achievement, is healthy for democracy.

✓ Connecting council staff and members with the electorate
through engagement exercises such as walking tours or
youth parliaments contributes to improved accountability
and invests in the next generation of leaders.

8

Corporate assets and resources

With a third of carbon emissions coming from our buildings, giving them a green makeover is supremely good for the planet and for the public purse (Boris Johnson, Mayor of London, UK, 2010, outlining plans to save US$773 million from sustainable procurement in public buildings).

Typical sustainability actions and outcomes	Cost-neutral interventions
8.1 Intelligent finance	#4, #15
8.2 Estates management	#53, #54, #55, #56, #57, #58, #59, #16
8.3 Procurement and whole-life costing	#17, #18, #60, #61, #62, #19
8.4 Staff compliance and champions	#63, #64, #65, #20 ,#21

8.1 **Intelligent finance**

Every second of every hour of every day or every year, councils and other organisations around the world are throwing away money from careless use of energy, water and other resources. For your council this may be as much as hundreds of thousands or even millions of

US dollars a year that could be better used to plug bulging gaps in your public spending budgets. Inefficiencies vary from wasting scarce resources (e.g. a building that needlessly loses heat) to poor use of one's assets (e.g. the failure to retrofit such buildings).

But what options are open to you if you have exhausted all avenues for any possible grant assistance or investments to effect improvements? One route is intelligent finance. So how does this work?

As we learnt from Woking Council in the UK, having the finance director engaged in sustainability means that more than half the battle is won in terms of building the business case to act in the first place. So, thinking about how your council's corporate asset and resources strategy links to sustainability priorities, if at all, also means being intelligent in how you can get your projects financed—especially if it can result in a cost-neutral intervention.

This intelligent finance may take a number of forms. One way is an in-house 'pay as you save fund' (PAYS) or 'revolving fund' which operates as an internal loan scheme where you borrow money to fund energy or water efficiency technologies, which is then repaid from the utility savings made as a result. The payback period for these types of investment tends to be reasonably short, and commonly between one and five years. One such scheme has been running successfully in Nillumbik, Australia, to fund water conservation investments—a sustainability issue of major concern to the council.

[#4] **Revolving funding for water conservation: Nillumbik Shire Council, Australia**

Located on the outskirts of Melbourne, the Shire of Nillumbik forms part of a north-eastern metropolitan green wedge: bounded by the Yarra River and the Kinglake Ranges. The shire has a population of just over 60,000 people who live in close-knit communities which range from typical urban settings to remote and tranquil bush properties. It is a comparatively affluent community in terms of income, health and well-being. Key industries include farming and tourism.

Owing to its hot and dry climate, in 2009 about 25% of the shire was affected by bushfire and there was serious loss of life and property. So a priority over the past 12 months has been, and will be over the next three or more years, bushfire environmental recovery and preparations for the annual summer fire period. This cost in the order of US$6.5 million for the previous year alone.

Nillumbik has benefited, however, from the fact that the country was not as exposed as Europe and North America to the global banking crisis and has been able to access national 'stimulus package' funding totalling US$3.7 million to upgrade facilities, buildings and recreational trails.

More widely, according to the council, Nillumbik has been recognised nationally for its environmental programmes including the way in which they are integrated into its core policy development activities, such as bushfire recovery and roadside hazards, erosion control, weed management and water catchment management. This complements other work in relation to waste exchange and recycling such as for kitchen food, computers and mobile phones; and energy efficiency and climate protection such as the retrofitting of street lighting and purchase of 100% green power, reducing greenhouse gas emissions by as much as 44%. The council also places a strong emphasis on the behavioural change work of a cross-departmental Eco Team, informing staff and the community alike through education programmes and marketing about the relevance of sustainability schemes to the people of Nillumbik (e.g. signage, media releases, community bulletins, information sessions and environmental events).

Commenting on the importance of Nillumbik's financial mechanisms for natural resource use, Margaret Abbey, the council's Group Manager, Environment and Planning Services, says:

> We are looking at getting a greater benefit from our 'revolving funds' where water and energy savings from building retrofits are returned to fund additional works. The other element is that we are looking at projects which provide a shorter payback period; and those which have a low cost for implementation, but still provide for improved environmental performance.

Having experienced drought for the past ten years in addition to state government-enforced water restrictions, such mechanisms are considered helpful to implementing the council's Sustainable

Water Management Plan. The purpose of the plan is to provide a strategic direction for improved water management throughout council operations and the Nillumbik community.

The plan has been developed to align with global best practice using guidelines set out in the ICLEI—Local Governments for Sustainability Water Campaign.

In terms of its own water use the council aims to achieve a 45% reduction (from 2000–2001 levels) by 2011. Since 2000, it has already achieved 35% reduction. This constituted a net saving of approximately US$40,000.

The plan aims to improve water management practices through:

- Education and behaviour change programmes within the council and the community

- Phased retrofit of council buildings with water-efficient devices

- Staged implementation of water-efficient practices in open space management

- The strategic development and implementation of guidelines that support water conservation and water quality management

Council operation actions to achieve this goal include:

- No irrigation of parkland

- Use of indigenous plant species in new amenity plantings

- Water conservation audits completed on priority council buildings

- Rain sensors and electronic irrigation system installed at its community environment centre

- Rainwater tank installed at pre-schools, community facilities and at its environment centre for use in toilet flushing

- Drought-tolerant grass species installed on all golf fairways as part of a wider water management plan for its golf course

- Re-use of pool and dam water in road grading operations

- Conduct of regular irrigation system audits and maintenance

- Connection of backwash system from swimming pool to sewer

- Water-sensitive urban design features incorporated into offices, leisure centres and road works

- Warm season grasses and subsurface drip irrigation installed at priority sporting fields

The above council-centric actions will complement other council-led community actions.

For further information visit www.nillumbik.vic.gov.au (accessed 15 September 2010).

This example from Nillumbik clearly showcases the value of a revolving fund for water. It demonstrates the ability to achieve life-changing services through this type of fund—and how important intelligent finance can be in achieving more with less—if you are smart. There are other corporate PAYS funds in operation for energy, too, which we will explore in Section 8.2 with a model used by North East Lincolnshire Council in the UK. (We examine *residential* options for PAYS in Chapter 12 in respect of a community management example from Berlin, Germany.)

If your council does not operate such a scheme, why not speak to the finance director about piloting it within prudent borrowing constraints? But again, many actions require no capital investment at all with the change coming down to that of behaviour, as has been proven through the actions seen above in Montgomery, Caracas and Ekurhuleni.

There are other financial alternatives that may be open to your council. One, for instance, is a carbon compensation levy that is charged to builders for all new developments, which is then reinvested in carbon reduction developments (efficiency or renewable) elsewhere in your authority, as is the case with Milton Keynes Council in the UK, which is described in Chapter 9. This is because it relates to private developments as opposed to council estates. However, there is no reason why you cannot change the terms of the levy policy to suit, is there? That is, the levy is then used to invest in your estates as well as community programmes.

Another route could be available via your public pension fund provider. This is in respect of an investment house financing a major district heating as a for-profit joint venture (however, while this is useful it is beyond the scope of this book given that the criteria are cost-neutral actions that are either free or have a short payback period).

Public pensions are interesting for another reason, too; how a council influences the investment strategy on sustainability matters is another way one can have a major impact. For example, local authorities in Connecticut and elsewhere in the USA are trying to tackle corporate greed in the wake of the bank bailouts (Social Investment Forum 2009). The 'say-on-pay' campaign is a brave attempt to stop banking and other corporate executives awarding themselves undeserved and risk-inducing, huge pay rises. While this may not at first appear to be a close-to-home issue, remember it is because of the debt burden of such bailouts that your council may face a huge drop in spending!

[#15] **Socially responsible investing in California and Connecticut, USA**

A concerted effort by local government pension funds with socially responsible investors, labour unions, religious investors and others for 'say-on-pay' executive compensation advisory votes at major US corporations came to a head during 2009. Of the recorded 100 companies facing 'say-on-pay' shareholder resolutions that year, five have recently agreed to schedule advisory votes.

The list of 100 companies includes 14 companies that will be required under the new federal stimulus bill to put such binding votes in place within one year, according to the Social Investment Forum (including household brand names such as American

Express). Earlier in 2009 American Express committed to implement the executive-compensation vote as required by President Obama's signing of the American Recovery and Reinvestment Act into law in 2009. This early action is expected to put pressure on other bailout fund recipients and, more broadly, leading non-banking companies, to embrace the 'say-on-pay' advisory vote as standard corporate practice.

Social Investment Forum CEO Lisa Woll synthesised this:

> The say-on-pay movement shows what concerned investors can do when they put their financial clout to work together. This unique investor network started in 2007—comprised of many socially responsible investors, public pension funds, labor funds, asset managers, foundations and religious investors. It is organised by the American Federation of State, County and Municipal Employees (AFSCME) Employees Pension Plan and Walden Asset Management, a division of Boston Trust and Investment Management Company.

'Say-on-pay' vote proponents are seeking a management-sponsored, non-binding advisory vote on executive compensation presented in the annual proxy statement. The resolutions have been submitted at a wide range of companies, including but not limited to those where pay has been excessive or where there has been a perceived misalignment between pay and performance over the past three to five years.

In 2009 campaign filings at major companies include Apple, American Express, Coca-Cola, AIG, Capital One, Hewlett-Packard, Intel, Wells Fargo, AT&T, Exxon Mobil, Raytheon, General Electric, Goldman Sachs, Home Depot, IBM, Merck, Time Warner, Citigroup, ConocoPhillips and Wal-Mart.

Aflac was the first US company to give shareholders a 'say-on-pay' vote in 2008, and it was overwhelmingly supported by over 95% of shareholders.

Proponents of the 2009 say-on-pay resolutions include public pension funds such as: California Public Employees' Retirement System (CalPERS), Connecticut Retirement Plans and Trust Funds (CRPTF) and New York City Pension Funds.

Remember, you have a right, if not an obligation, to ask. After all, you are a client of this investment house and it is your money! Similar principles should apply to how you approach investing any council reserves.

Having now looked at intelligent finance we must consider the advances which can be achieved through managing the footprint of council estates.

8.2 Estates management

Over time, all councils will design, construct or occupy buildings for its corporate business, whether for office administration or community use such as leisure centres or schools.

Applied research about advanced buildings of the future (Caddet 1995; De Montfort University 2010) suggests there should be several motivating factors for one to act:

- Building regulations

- Cost

- Comfort

- Concern for the environment

- Energy independence

- Sustainable use of resources

The weight attached to each of these factors will vary from nation to nation (notably in terms of building regulations) as well as best practice on voluntary sustainability standards in construction such as LEED (USA), R2000 (Canada), PassivHaus (Europe) and BREEAM (UK), which look into issues ranging from management construction, health and well-being, pollution, transport, land use, ecology, materials and water. And this is all part of your business case, of course!

Regardless of whether these exist in your country or not, observing a sustainability hierarchy affords the opportunity to save money as well as the planet. This relates to our next tip below.

[#53] Avoiding the temptation of fool's gold

One word of warning is to avoid the lure of 'fool's gold' that can sometimes be the rush to install micro-renewables first, simply because it is the 'sexier' end of the market.

Instead, reduce the footprint of the building through its upfront design first through the adoption of energy or water efficient approaches and materials (e.g. super-insulation through triple-glazed windows). Then consider how the building is used once occupied, such as through building controls to avoid unnecessary use (e.g. artificial light timers). Finally you should look to source utilities from appropriate local and/or renewable sources (De Montfort University 2010). This hierarchy is detailed in Figure 8.2.1.

FIGURE 8.2.1 **Hierarchy for reducing the footprint of a building**

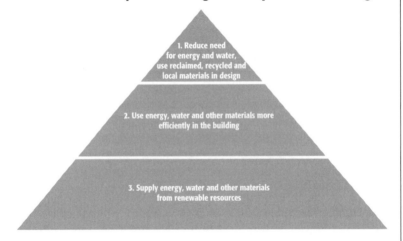

In reality, however, your opportunity to intervene will depend on the status of the building. That is, is it yet to be built or are you an occupying tenant? Is it modern and fitted out with the latest sustainability features or is it an old building that needs to be retrofitted? Also, do you own or lease the building and what influence and/or control do you have over modifications?

If you are a tenant rather than an owner-occupier, then by and large, the landlord will agree to you investing in sustainability measures given it improves the value of the asset. (Remember to get written permission that this is acceptable and that you do not have to return the building to its original less sustainable state upon your departure from the building!) Ideally, the landlord would also pay for or co-invest in these modifications.

Given the focus of this book, however, we will again focus attention on high-impact, cost-neutral actions one can take with a relatively short payback period. So, in terms of operating costs, the 'big ticket' opportunities here primarily relate to energy followed by water and the sustainable procurement of materials such as paper, stationery or food that leads to waste. This is because these tend to account for a significant proportion of the estates budget to the tune of hundreds of thousands or millions of US dollars each year and there is scope to take significant action. As we covered corporate water in detail in the Nillumbik case study, we now turn to energy and then sustainable procurement consecutively.

So starting at the top of the hierarchy from the 'fool's good' tip above, in terms of reducing the need for energy in building design, we first need to understand how energy is both used and lost in a typical non-domestic or commercial building (demonstrated in Fig. 8.2.2 with data from the UK). However, it must be remembered that the exact energy needs will depend on the specific office use as well as the local climate. The latter can be linked to certain factors such as: geographical latitude, season of the year, altitude and topography, effects of water and atmospheric circulation (McMullan 2007). While the UK is deemed a temperate climate, other climates are characterised as either cold (e.g. Chicago, USA), hot/dry (e.g. Riyadh, Saudi Arabia) or warm/humid (e.g. Macau, China).

From Figure 8.2.2 we can see that space and water heating is the major area of use, followed by ventilation and lighting. And as illustrated in Figure 8.2.3, heat loss arises from floors, walls, roofs, windows and ventilation. Consequently these are the aspects that are honed in on now.

FIGURE 8.2.2 **Typical UK air-conditioned office energy usage**

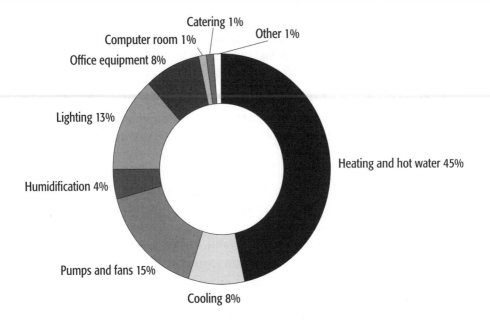

FIGURE 8.2.3 **Sources of heat loss from an office building**

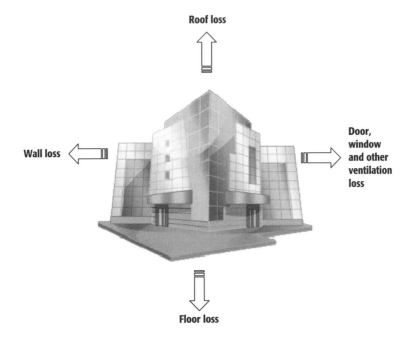

Again, the exact breakdown of loss will depend on the design, but also the materials used in respect of their thermal conductivity or insulation properties, which in turn will be informed by the density of the said material. So, for instance, in terms of walls, concrete block has a lower thermal conductivity value than brickwork so insulates better. This brings us to the importance of selecting materials that will best prevent/allow heat loss, according your local climate needs (CIBSE 2006).

[#54] Thermal conductivity of typical building materials

Material	Density (kg/m³)	Thermal conductivity (W/mK)
WALLS (EXTERNAL AND INTERNAL)		
Asbestos cement sheet	700	0.36
Asbestos cement decking	1,500	0.36
Brickwork (outer leaf)	1,700	0.84
Brickwork (inner leaf)	1,700	0.62
Cast concrete (dense)	2,000	1.30
Cast concrete (lightweight, dry)	770	0.22
Concrete block (heavy weight)	2,240	1.31
Concrete block (medium weight)	970	0.32
Concrete block (aerated)	750	0.24
Plasterboard, gypsum	800	0.16
SURFACE FINISHES		
External rendering, dry	1,430	1.13
Cement plaster	1,760	0.72
ROOFS		
Aerated concrete slab	500	0.16
Asphalt	1,700	0.50
Felt/bitumen layers	1,700	0.85
Screed	1,200	0.41
Stone chippings	1,800	0.96
Tile, clay	1,890	0.80
FLOORS		
Cast concrete (dense)	2,200	1.70
Timber flooring	650	0.14
Wood block	650	0.14

Material	Density (kg/m³)	Thermal conductivity (W/mK)
INSULATION		
Expanded polystyrene slab	23	0.04
Glass fibre quilt	12	0.04
Glass fibre slab	25	0.04
Mineral fibre blanket	24	0.04
Urea formaldehyde	10	0.04
Polyisocyanate	45	0.03

Remember, nearly all building walls, floors and roofs consist of several layers of different materials, so to calculate the overall conduction or insulation properties you need to consider the combined influence.

Good day lighting is also a key ally in your battle to save energy in non-domestic buildings as it reduces the electrical consumption of the lighting. In addition, it also reduces the internal heat gains from artificial lighting and in air-conditioned buildings this reduced heat gain means that less cooling is needed. And so this brings us to embrace a 'passive' building approach: a building in which a comfortable interior climate can be maintained without active heating and cooling systems.

[#55] **Become passive!**

How many times have you been in a meeting room with the blinds drawn when it is sunny outside but the lights are on in the room? Or when there were lights on when you entered the room but it was empty? Well, this is obviously a complete waste of money not to mention a pretty unpleasant environment!

Passive building design can overcome this. Key principles include:

- The potential for solar gain through siting and site layout. In a cold or temperate climate building orientation is made to maximise solar gain; vice versa in a warm climate

- Building form. The lower the exposed envelope area, the lower the heat loss

- Internal planning. Zoning different spaces to make best use of solar gain such as meeting rooms as opposed to kitchen space which will already get heat gain from appliances

- Glazing. Multiple glazing of windows and doors

- Shading. Using shutters or curtains to prevent overheating while taking advantage of natural daylight

- Ventilation and airtightness. Temperatures can be moderated by ventilating the property at night to cool the office prior to the next warm day in summer or controlled ventilation via small windows to reduce heat loss in the winter

- Control systems. A 'responsive heating and lighting system' (such as thermostatic radiator valves in each meeting room) takes advantage of any localised solar gain as well as timer light controls to avoid excessive use

But what does this mean in terms of cost reduction and carbon savings? Siting and layout considerations and reducing the thermostat by just 1°C through a responsive heating system taken together can immediately benefit you and save up to 15% of annual heating demand. Big stuff (De Montfort University 2010)![1]

These passive principles can be applied to existing as well as new properties. Take for instance the painting of external surfaces as part of routine maintenance. Leaving corporate colour to one side for the moment, painting surfaces in line with energy requirements surely makes more sense?

---

1 See also Energy Saving Trust, www.est.org.uk, accessed April 2010.

[#56] **Painting the town white (or black)**

Amazingly, according to new research, painting surfaces white in hot climates and black in cold climates can significantly reduce heating demand in buildings. According to Professor Steven Chu, Nobel Prize-winning physicist and US Energy Secretary (Gray 2009):

> If you look at all the buildings and if you make the roofs white and if you make the pavement more of a concrete type of colour rather than a black type of colour and if you do that uniformly, that would be the equivalent of . . . reducing the carbon emissions due to all the cars in the world by 11 years.

Professor Chu calculates that painting the roofs of homes in hot countries white would save energy and money on air conditioning by deflecting the sun's rays. White roofs can cut indoor temperatures by up to 20°C, reducing the need for energy-intensive cooling systems. More pale surfaces could also slow global warming by reflecting heat into space rather than allowing it to be absorbed by dark surfaces from where it is trapped by greenhouse gases and increases temperatures.

Taking this a step further are students at the Massachusetts Institute of Technology who have developed a roof tile that turns white in the heat of the sun, reflecting its rays back into space, the latest techno-fix solution for cooling the planet (Howarth 2010). When the weather is cold the 'Thermeleon' slate remains black.

Of course, you cannot always rely on natural light (for instance, if weather conditions are overcast or you are operating at night-time) and so artificial lighting will then become essential in terms of selecting the right type of lamp and controlling it in the right way.

For some lamps it is more important to choose a highly luminous product (e.g. roadways). For others, it is about the right type of colour for working (e.g. for shop window displays). Selecting the right product can account for 13% of your energy bill so you need to get this right. Table 8.2 and the next tip have more information.

TABLE 8.2 **Characteristics of electric lamps**

Type	Wattage	Luminous efficacy (lm/W)	Life (hours)	Colour temperature (K)	Applications
Tungsten filament	40–200	12	1,000	2,700	Homes, hotels, cafes
Tungsten halogen	300–2,000	25	2,000–4,000	2,800–3,000	Area and display lighting
Compact fluorescent	9–20	60	8,000+	3,000	Homes, offices and public buildings
Tubular fluorescent	20–125	80	8,000+	3,000–6,500	Offices and shops
Mercury fluorescent	50–2,000	60	8,000+	4,000	Factories and roadways
Mercury halide	240–3,500	70	8,000+	3,000–6,500	Offices and shops
High-pressure sodium	70–1,000	125	8,000+	2,100	Factories and roadways
Low-pressure sodium	35–180	180	8,000+	not applicable	Roadways and area lighting

Source: McMullan 2007

As you can see from Table 8.2, higher-wattage lamps generally have higher efficiency and a longer life. So, for councils, the most appropriate lamp is likely to be tubular or compact fluorescent for administrative office work, schools or public function rooms; with mercury fluorescent or high-pressure sodium lamps for the workshop of an in-house fleet, as well as low-pressure sodium lamps for area lighting.

And, according to Brown (2009), the good news is that the lighting sector is on the edge of an amazing technological advancement with the light-emitting diode (LED), which uses up to 85% less electricity than an incandescent light bulb and lasts 50 times longer, too. The relatively high cost of LEDs is dropping fast and if it continues to do so, says Brown, then it will make widespread use feasible (and beyond current niche markets such as traffic lights).

Of course now you have installed the right lighting you need to use it in the most effective way. So your choice of lighting control strategy is imperative. This is illustrated opposite. Again, for councils, appropriate lighting controls may be time switching for a busy administrative office, localised switching in meeting rooms and photoelectric switching for area lighting in rarely visited locations which may be needed for safety reasons to avoid incidents of crime.

Having looked at both design and operational options, finally, we need to turn attention to the end of the hierarchy to examine possibilities for alternative energy, that is, renewable energy.

Earlier in the book we touched on 'peak oil' being reached in 2015, so for energy security purposes alone, local councils need to look at all options for maintaining a quality supply of energy to continue to deliver services to communities. Renewables can assist with this. The major types of non-fossil-fuel energy source include:

- Solar. Energy direct from the sun captured by special pipes or panels for hot water heating or electricity

- Wind. Energy captured using wind turbines or mills onshore or offshore

- Wave. Energy captured using sea devices that rise and fall with the tide

- Hydro. Energy from falling water using turbines

[#57] Lighting control choices

Occupancy patterns		Lighting control strategy			
NUMBER OF PEOPLE	TIME	TIME SWITCHING	LOCALISED SWITCHING	OCCUPANCY LINKING	PHOTOELECTRIC DAYLIGHT LINK
IF DAYLIGHT AVAILABLE					
Many people	Variable	●●●		●	●
	Intermittent but regular	●●●	●	●	●
	Continuous	●●●	●●	Not applicable	●●●
A few people	Variable	●	●●●	●●	●
	Continuous	●	●●●	Not applicable	●●
Rarely occupied	Intermittent	●	●●	●●●	●
NO DAYLIGHT					
All types of occupancy		●●●	Not applicable	●●●	Not applicable

Key: ●●● = most appropriate; ● = least appropriate

Source: BRE 1994

- Geothermal. Energy from the heat of the Earth, captured as hot water or steam

- Biofuels. Energy made from the burning of wood, food or other biowaste

But what type of fuel is most suitable? And what is the best way to develop this capacity? We look at this next.

[#58] **Yes, renewables. But which kind?**

Your choice of renewable energy source will be informed by a number of factors. In terms of securing a supply of renewable energy for heating space and water and for electricity a council has a number of options:

- Procuring a so-called 'green tariff' from a recognised distributor

- On-site generation by the council itself

- Partnering with other major energy users to develop a district heating scheme

- A combination of all of the above

The decision on the most appropriate option should be shaped by a number of factors, notably:

- Availability. Determined by the local environment (e.g. solar in a hot/dry climate or in a humid climate hydro may be more desirable)

- Cost. Buying in the green tariff versus investment in self-generation

- Reliability. Whether the technology is dependent on certain weather conditions or provides enough energy to meet your needs

- Control. The extent to which the council governs distribution of the energy

- Complementary technologies. Ensuring your selection of multiple technologies does not result in one detracting from another (e.g. air/ground source heat pumps 'competing' with combined heat and power)

- Financial incentives. Are you punished for using carbon (e.g. permits for purchase in the UK) or rewarded for generating renewables (e.g. feed-in tariffs in Germany)

The answers to all these questions will vary according to a council's particular context again. The costs associated with these schemes (which can run into millions of dollars) and the length of the payback period (which is usually much longer than five years) means that detailed recommendations are beyond the scope of this book. Having said this, it should be noted that there are market interventions a council can make to encourage such developments from the local marketplace through business support and planning policy (explored further in Chapter 9).

Should you wish to pursue renewables, we would offer three cautionary points.

First, it makes more financial sense to co-invest with partners in a district heating scheme given the economy of scale involved and the advantage of sharing the burden of risk. Increasingly, councils are looking to enjoy the benefit from district heating schemes, such as in the form of a combined heat and power (CHP) plant, as is the case with Gothenburg City, Sweden (LGA 2009). District heating schemes such as this are viable because of the heat demand from other local major energy users such as hospitals, schools and residential areas and this has a number of advantages from an energy and carbon viewpoint. A CHP plant is more energy-efficient (80%) than fossil fuel plants (30%) as, normally, when fuel is burnt to make electricity lots of heat is lost to the atmosphere. However, because CHP is generated locally less is lost in transmission and it can recycled to warm water or even to help cool the building (Vitali Energy 2007). CHP plants can often be bi-generation, which means they can accept both gas and biomass, allowing for any unexpected supply chain disruptions.

Second, and just as importantly, such district heating schemes need to be future-proofed and part of any new so-called 'smart grid' being rolled out. This sophisticated, low-carbon distribution network allows generators to sell surplus energy back to the national grid, to recharge plug-in hybrid electric vehicles used by its residents, as well as make use of smart meter display units to help building owners or managers better control energy supply and demand. One successful local authority example is Boulder, USA (US Department of Energy 2010).

Third, procuring a green tariff for a distributor does not necessarily solve your energy security problem unless you are able to gain assurances over the quality and reliability of that supply source. Some suppliers have also been known to market a fuel as a green tariff when in fact renewables only account for a portion of the said product.

Pulling this all together lends itself to another suggestion: that is, selecting the appropriate built environment features for a particular climate type (see opposite; based on McMullan 2007).

The list given here is intended to be illustrative not exhaustive. Local features will strongly influence choices, too: for instance, if you are fortunate enough to have an abundance of local forests then timber will be a primary choice of construction material, and a potential power source in terms of biofuels. To make this slightly more complex, you will also need to consider the interactions of different environmental decisions. For instance, an increased window area will offer more heat loss and gain as well as more daylight but will also lead to more noise intrusion.

Further reading on sources of ideas on green and sustainable buildings is contained at the end of this book.

However, while this is all very well in theory, what about in practice? Through a PAYS carbon management programme, North East Lincolnshire Council is working to save millions of dollars over a period of five years or less (see page 90).

[#59] Connecting the natural and built environment

Climate type	Natural environment	Built environment
Hot/dry	• Overheating for most of year • Dry air allows evaporation • Temperature ranges −10°C to 45°C • High radiation • Strong winds	• Light-coloured surfaces • Roof overhang to provide shade • Opening for breezes • Courtyards to trap cool air • Smaller windows to avoid solar gain • Solar, wind power
Warm/humid	• Overheating for most of year • Humid air inhibits cooling • Temperature often above 20°C • Mean relative humidity 80% • High rainfall in certain months	• Lightweight materials, e.g. timber • Building on stilts for ventilation • Rainwater harvesting • Hydro, biofuels power
Temperate	• Excessive heat loss part of year • Inadequate heat loss part of year • Temperate ranges −30°C to 30°C • Precipitation in all seasons	• High insulation, e.g. double glazing • Tightly sealed construction • Mechanical ventilation, heat recovery • Larger windows for natural light • Efficient heating, lighting with controls • Responsive heating with thermostat • Biofuels, wind or wave power
Cold	• Excessive heat loss most of year • Minimum temperatures below −15°C	• Dark-coloured surfaces • Heavyweight materials, e.g. recycled concrete (or a low-carbon alternative) • Super-insulation, e.g. triple-glazing • Tightly sealed construction • Mechanical ventilation, heat recovery • Efficient heating, lighting with controls • Geothermal, wind power

Source: based on McMullen 2007

[#16] **Counting the carbon and the cash in North East Lincolnshire, UK**

Since 2008, North East Lincolnshire Council has been working in partnership with the national support agency the Carbon Trust to identify a range of carbon and cost savings that will enable it to meet its carbon reduction target of 25% by 2013 from 2008 (North East Lincolnshire Council 2009).

A Carbon Management Plan (CMP) has been adopted that includes projects to reduce the council's carbon emissions from council estates, transport, schools and involving all employees through awareness raising and behaviour change.

The council will make the carbon reductions through the following actions, among other things:

- The council and schools work together to identify energy-saving measures during their refurbishment, such as energy-efficient lighting, heating control and zoning and efficient boilers. This is important as schools are a major source of emissions

- Driver training has been delivered to staff who operate refuse trucks. The training helps to drive down operating costs, fuel consumption and carbon emissions (as well as aiding safe and efficient driving)

- All new fleet vehicles use the latest engine technology, complying with the stringent Euro V standards

- The council has been advocating the benefits of car sharing, public transport, walking and cycling to employees for business and personal travel

- Light-emitting diodes (LEDs) in bollards, lanterns and illumination are used by the council to incorporate energy saving measures

All of this is enabling the council to make financial savings of US$8.55 million based on an outlay of US$0.75 million, with the investment budget drawn from a match of internal PAYS funds and an interest-free loan from the national government.

This complements wider community-based work to reduce the council's carbon footprint such as through the use of landfill (a major source of methane, a powerful greenhouse gas). By providing a comprehensive range of recycling and composting facilities across North East Lincolnshire and by recovering the energy from household waste to produce electricity and hot water, the council has been able to substantially reduce the amount of waste that goes to landfill.

So like Nillumbik, North East Lincolnshire Council is using intelligent finance to restore its estates portfolio and make it more sustainable. And remember, even if you do not currently have the in-house skills to develop a carbon management plan, you can factor in the cost of sourcing external help to your PAYS scheme! There really is no reason why you cannot make this happen. So go for it!

Next we look at the role of flexible procurement.

8.3 **Procurement and whole-life costing**

Council procurement is one of the most powerful tools at your disposal to influence sustainability outcomes, as we have already seen in Montgomery County Government's efforts to green its office operations through to Nillumbik Shire Council's measures on water conservation.

How so? Every year your council will spend millions and sometimes billions of dollars on capital projects and goods and services, ranging from computers and stationery to hotel accommodation and vehicles for hire. Given the amounts of public money involved and to ensure probity, there are often strict rules or a framework to guide how such goods and services should be procured in a fair, transparent and competitive manner; especially in terms of securing the lowest possible prices.

Simultaneously, the business case for a flexible approach can also be supported and this involves consideration of 'whole-life costing', a technique to establish the total cost of ownership. It is a structured approach that addresses all the elements of this cost and can be used to produce a spend profile of the product or service over its anticipated life-span. The results can be used to assist management in the decision-making process where there is a choice of options. That is, to examine *value for money* as opposed to just the *lowest price*.

Looking at this through a sustainability lens, simply, this means adding in additional social and environmental criteria to sit alongside the existing economic ones, such as buying locally to stimulate local trade, reducing CO_2 emissions and/or waste to landfill, eliminating child labour or supporting opportunities for the long-term unemployed. Below is a detailed example on the procurement of a particular council road maintenance product. As you can see, there was no cost involved in doing any of this beyond staff time from the procurement team but it still yielded real financial savings among other benefits.

[#17] **Whole-life costing to improve health and safety in Wakefield, UK**

Wakefield Council traditionally used pre-cast concreted kerb edgings when building or maintaining its 1,400 km road network. As the laying of traditional kerb by hand involves a risk of injury to the workforce, so the council took steps to reduce this risk but also examined the options for other supplementary benefits (Wakefield Council 2009).

A trial was undertaken to use lightweight kerbside edgings made entirely from recycled materials and was chosen as it reduced the installation costs and time, it lessened the risk of harm and it met the council's commitments to reduce carbon emissions and to make more use of recycled materials.

Wakefield selected a product called Durakerb, which is made entirely from recycled materials. It is laid in a similar manner as the traditional product, but has many additional advantages. The comparative assessment is as summarised in the table opposite.

In conclusion, while the unit cost of Durakerb is greater than the traditional product, when additional whole-life costs (such as the expense of machinery, labour and sickness absence) are all factored in it represents a 5% saving. At the same time staff welfare has increased and carbon emissions have been reduced. Everyone is a winner!

	Durakerb	Traditional	Comparison
TRANSPORTATION			
Loads per 38 tonne trailer	1,248 units	364 units	3.4 times greater load
Weight of load	6.7 tonnes	25.1 tonnes	73% lighter
CO_2 emissions*	247 kg CO_2e		
PRODUCTION			
Use of raw materials	0%	100%	Total saving
Purchase cost per unit	US$12.87	US$3.84	3.4 times more expensive
Embodied carbon (manufacture)	8.7 kg but recyclable	10.5 kg	17% lower
INSTALLATION**			
Installer labour, 2 persons	US$274 per person per day	US$274 per person per day	Same
Mechanical lifter	Not applicable	US$25	Total saving
Lorry and driver	Not applicable	US$378	Total saving
Days to install 325 m	1.30	4.06	3 times quicker
Damage rate	1%	5%	80% less damage
Installation costs	US$11,287	US$11,954	US$668 or 5% saving

*   Based on a 15 tonne Euro 5 lorry travelling 100 km; kgCO_2e is the total carbon dioxide equivalent emitted in kg

** 325 m, based on installation cost of US$10 of linear metre of bedding material

This is becoming an increasingly mature professional area of work in the field of procurement as evidenced by a range of ISO standards on both product life-cycle assessment and environmental labelling: 14040, 14041, 14042, 14043 and 14020, 14021, 14022, 14023, 14024, 14025, respectively. All of which complements and builds on longstanding consumer-driven campaigns with mandatory or voluntary schemes from government or non-governmental organisations (NGOs) and others such as the EU's Eugene Standard, the USA's Energy Star label, and the Humane Cosmetics Standard and Fairtrade logo, respectively.

This plethora of purchasing codes and market offerings has left many procurement teams in local government bamboozled over which ones to use. Subsequently, a number of advocates have stepped forward to provide practical guidance on how to shape the quality of the agenda; see for instance the Responsible Purchasing Network by the Center for a New American Dream, which boasts hundreds of local councils as participants (including the City of Austin and Santa Monica which we will share very shortly). The Center even has a green calculator so you can compare and contrast the costs and benefits from the market options.

Some national governments have also gone a step further along this road to stipulate *how* public sector buyers should prioritise areas for consideration on sustainability matters, given both the known levels of spend and a phased approach for successful implementation. This is intended to help local authorities navigate the sometimes complex, legal world of procurement to overcome any perceived barriers. For example, in the UK the concept of sustainable procurement is defined as:

> A process whereby organisations meet their needs for goods, services, works and utilities in a way that achieves value for money on a whole life basis in terms of generating benefits not only to the organisation but also to society and the economy, while minimising damage to the environment (OGC 2007).

As part of this all local councils are asked to specifically look at the top ten spend priorities of:

- Construction (building and refit, highways and local roads, operations and maintenance)
- Health and social work (operating costs of hospitals, care homes, social care provision)
- Food
- Uniforms, clothing and other textiles
- Water
- Pulp, paper and printing

- Energy

- Consumable (office machinery and computers)

- Furniture

- Transport (business travel, motor vehicles)

Of course, again, the relevant areas of focus will depend on the council's remit as determined by national law and local conditions.

Bringing this learning together there are common features which one can use to develop a universal, generic approach to guide sustainable procurement as shown in Figure 8.3 (OGC 2007; Responsible Purchasing Network 2010).

FIGURE 8.3 **Step change on sustainable procurement**

Step 1
- Appoint a senior champion for sustainable procurement
- Form a technical group to project-manage, and review whole-life costing

Step 2
- Identify issues, opportunities and risk on key expenditure, collect baseline data
- Develop new procurement policy, endorsed by council CEO

Step 3
- Communicate policy to staff, suppliers and residents
- Do more in-depth training for key personnel, including setting goals

Step 4
- Key contracts start to include sustainability criteria
- Award on value for money not lowest price

Step 5
- Measure progress against policy objectives
- Evaluate effectiveness and any competence gaps

Step 6
- Further align and integrate as council strategy and operations evolve
- Align with environmental management systems, publish results and share learning

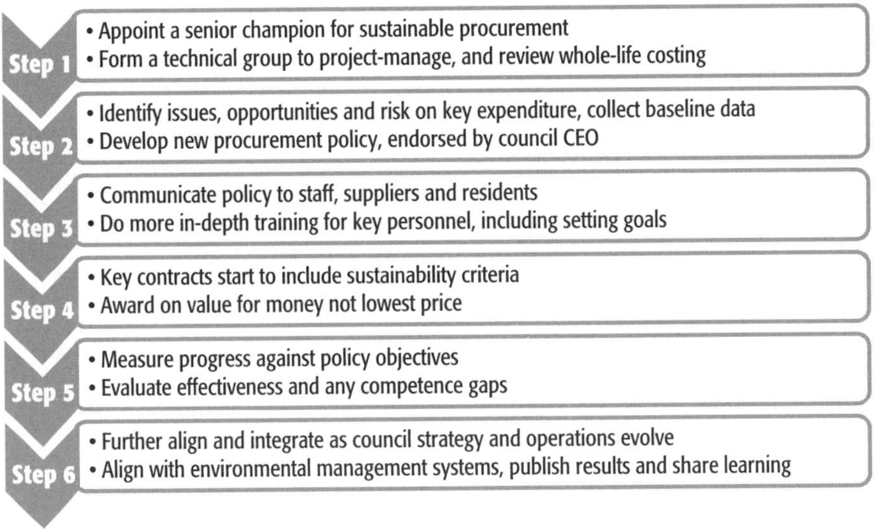

As is evident in Figure 8.3, the role of communications and training is fundamentally important here, something we will explore further in the next section.

So given all of this, what would be quick wins for you? Here are a range of procurement examples spanning carbon, waste, water and local employment for you to review your sustainability.

[#18] **Dollar and eco-savings from education on smart buying in Austin, USA**

For this Texan council it is all about education on proving the dollar savings and providing training for the transition to a green economy. Sustainable procurement work has reaped contract dividends in terms of decisions on: concentrated cleaning products, Energy Star-rated electronics, remanufactured printer cartridge multi-function printers, LED and CFL energy-efficient lamps and motion sensors for office lights.

Waste and water is a big issue for many, too, as we learnt from Nillumbik. Below are two related tips that have been put forward together. (Note, we will explore waste and environmental services for residents in more detail in Chapter 10.)

[#60, #61, #62] **Free the caged water, bin the garbage bins and catch the wasters**

Have you entered or left a meeting room where there are lots of half-empty plastic cups of water from the local cooler? Do you sometimes receive official council documents printed one side of the paper only? Have you observed that the office paper recycling bin often has sheets of paper inside it which have only been printed on one side?

Easy but effective solutions to these problems are to, first, replace all bottled water and water coolers with tap water; second, remove individual desk bins and relocate a central refuse bin to sit alongside the office recycling area to force behaviour change; and, third, ensure all computers and printers have a default function to print double-sided (you can still monitor major paper consumers by the print or photocopy codes to ensure there is no abuse of the system).

In addition to conserving water and minimising waste it will also reduce your carbon footprint by reducing the energy used in processing bottled water, so, a win, win, win situation!

These are all simple, free-to-do actions, which will save your council a lot of money.

Having said this, it may be that for environmental health reasons you are unable to drink tap water or because of technological impediments you cannot print double-sided. Not to worry for now; remember: it is all about doing the best you can in *your* particular circumstances and adapt accordingly. So, if people have printed on one side of paper, either ask them to re-use it for printing on the other side or as scrap notepaper.

For others, though, maintaining and creating local employment and skills through procurement is a much more important driver than 'classic' environmental savings, as is obviously the case in Santa Monica. Essentially this is about keeping money local and preventing it from leaking out of the authority.

[#19] **Buy local in the City of Santa Monica, USA**

'Buy Local Santa Monica' was created by representatives of the Santa Monica business community and the City of Santa Monica to support local businesses and raise awareness of the community, economic and environmental benefits of choosing local first.

Some of the key benefits according to Santa Monica are that:

- It keeps money in Santa Monica's economy, for every US$100 spent at a local business, US$45 stays in the community. Spending locally ensures that sales taxes are reinvested in Santa Monica

- It helps the environment, having a diverse range of businesses within walking or biking distance reduces the amount of driving citizens need to do, lessens traffic and air pollution and helps to conserve land

- It keeps and creates local jobs; studies show that locally owned businesses create more jobs in the community and often provide better wages and benefits than national chains

So, the task for your council is to analyse your major areas of spend to consider how you can identify quick wins, too.

All of which brings us to the final section of this chapter: some very important people—you and your colleagues!

8.4 **Staff compliance and champions**

As we have discussed, behaviour change is key—whether among the general public and council staff or elected members in relation to member inductions, freedom for officers to innovate, new training requirements on sustainable building design or flexible procurement. However, whatever you intentions you have, nothing tangible and meaningful will improve on sustainability matters without the effective management of staff.

FIGURE 8.4 **Staff advocacy or staff rules?**

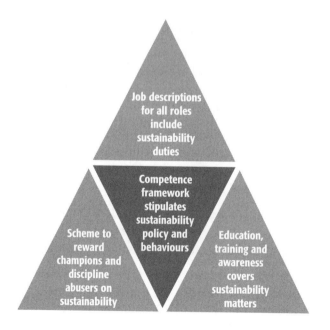

Critically, the right balance between compliance and advocacy is essential. This can take a number of important forms but, most vitally, it needs to be backed up through your personnel team with the approval of leadership and should encompass everything from corporate policy and role descriptions, through to staff training incentives or disciplinary schemes, as shown in Figure 8.4.

So, the obvious question that remains is why, for some local councils, is the efficient use of assets and resources by staff voluntary? We return to the issue of mandating later in Chapters 12 and 13. For now, we explore these elements through a series of examples, starting with sustainability 'duties' for all staff.

[#63, #64, #65] **Conditioning staff on air conditioning, jumpers and coffee breaks**

Have you ever been in an office when someone wearing a jumper is complaining about the heat and at the same time someone wearing a sleeveless shirt is complaining about the cold? Or when you go to the kitchen or canteen you have seen a half-full kettle boiling so one person can make just one cup of coffee? If the answer is, yes, then your council is wasting money yet again.

Easy remedies for this are as follows: first implement an air conditioning policy that complements your thermostat controls (as referenced earlier in the estates management section) so people are clear when it is acceptable to use air conditioning and when it is not; second, be clear with staff about what corrective action they can take, within boundaries, to stay warm or cool (e.g. choice of clothing); and, finally, notices on the walls in the kitchen should make it clear that it is a social taboo to make a hot drink just for yourself.

Having showed some examples of effective controls, we will now consider successful staff messaging campaigns in Rennes and Sydney.

[#20, #21] **Display days in Rennes, France; blackouts across Sydney, Australia**

Rennes Métropole uses an annual Display Day campaign to show-case to staff and residents alike how the council is benefiting from going green. The open days include tours of municipal buildings that are harnessing the latest energy-efficient and renewable tech-nology.[2]

Sydney has taken this messaging idea a step further by signing up to WWF's annual Earth Hour campaign which involves switch-ing off council lights during a one-hour blackout (Grist 2007).

Both campaigns in their different ways are important in get-ting members of staff to think about and appreciate the every-day impacts of their actions in terms of energy consumption and water, whether they agree with it or not. Remember: lots of coun-cil employees will also be council residents, so it is a double win to bring these people along with you!

So yet again, it can be seen there is tremendous scope to save money by investing staff time in changing attitudes. But determin-ing the right balance between carrot and stick is a real challenge. We have already seen in different ways how Nillumbik and Montgomery are both trying to force behaviour change on water conservation and green office operations, respectively. And in subsequent chapters we will consider others: for example, Knowsley Council in the UK requires its fleet team to drive in a smart way to save fuel and reduce carbon emissions simultaneously.

In the next chapter we will examine the crucial role played by eco-nomic development and planning departments in, among other things, changing the behaviour of businesses by intervening to provide clear market signals.

2 Covenant of Mayors, www.eumayors.eu, accessed April 2010.

Key learning

✓ Your corporate assets and resources play a pivotal role in advancing sustainability.

✓ Intelligent finance means you can make modest resources go far, such as water revolving funds.

✓ By strengthening your approach to estates management and its use of resources through a sustainability hierarchy, you can save money in terms of reduced running costs (notably with energy bills).

✓ Whole-life costing in procurement can help to realise the value for money of different purchasing options, such as reducing the incidence of sickness absence or improving environmental performance.

✓ But the role of HR in achieving staff support for or compliance with corporate policies on sustainability is critical to success.

9

Economic development and planning

California is showing the rest of the nation and the world that you can protect the environment and the economy at the same time (Arnold Schwarzenegger, Governor of California, 2010, after signing legislation to grow solar investment and create green jobs).

Typical sustainability actions and outcomes	Cost-neutral interventions
9.1 Land use and climate adaptation	#5, #66, #22
9.2 Low-carbon trade zones	#23, #67
9.3 Business incubation, signals and control	#68, #69, #70, #24
9.4 Green spaces infrastructure	#71, #25

9.1 Land use and climate adaptation

Council activities that help to attract inward investment, keep money local, generate wealth, create employment, develop the workforce, alleviate poverty and raise standards of living are, understandably, often viewed as the 'jewel in the crown' by leaders in local government and residents alike. Consequently, when it comes to the cost-neutral and high-impact interventions a council can make to effect sustainability change, economic development and planning is a primary pathway in terms of risks and opportunities.

To put this into context further, see Figure 9.1, which shows typical sources of GHG from various economic activities (*Stern Review* 2006).

FIGURE 9.1 **Greenhouse gas emissions by source**

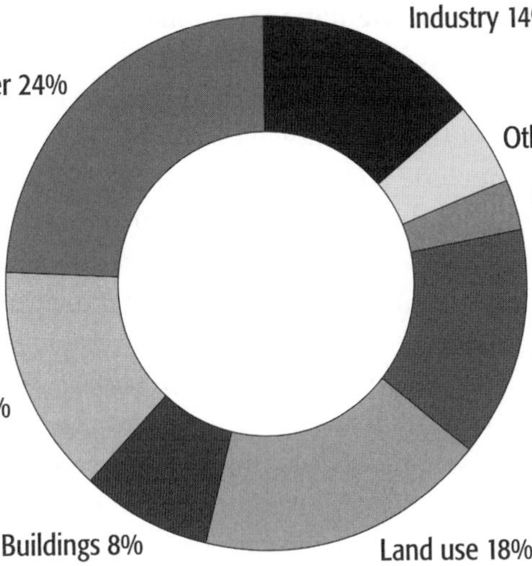

Industry 14%

Power 24%

Other energy-related 5%

Waste 3%

Agriculture 14%

Transport 14%

Buildings 8%

Land use 18%

Total emissions in 2000: 42 GtCO$_2$e

Of course, the emissions data will differ between local authorities depending on particular industries, technologies and population densities, and so this figure is simply intended to illustrate the challenge—to be prosperous without killing the planet.

With this in mind, the following chapter elaborates on how you can improve sustainability through land-use planning and climate adaptation, clean technology development, business support offerings, and the development of a green space strategy. Although selective, these themes focus attention on key areas of intervention on sustainability matters (rather than being an exhaustive list, as per the remit of this book). In addition to this, issues related to housing quality and sustainable living are to be picked up in Chapter 12 as part of your community management considerations.

To begin with, in this first section the focus will be on inclusive approaches to land-use planning, taking the case of the City of Ulaanbaatar in Mongolia and its novel approach to urban development as part of its participation in the UN Global Compact Cities Programme.

[#5] **Urban development through participation: City of Ulaanbaatar, Mongolia**

Located in north-central Mongolia, the City of Ulaanbaatar is the country's capital and largest city with a population of about 1 million, representing 40% of the national population. Once a city of nomads, during the 20th century it initially grew into a significant manufacturing centre and today prides itself as the nation's cultural and financial centre, too (Global Compact Cities Programme 2010). Key sectors include construction, mining (e.g. coal, copper and gold), oil, food and beverages and the processing of animal products (e.g. cashmere). It is a major transport hub as well given its connections to the Trans-Siberian Railway and the Chinese railway network.

Consequently, over recent years the population has rapidly grown as a result of significant rural–urban migration. Tens of thousands more arrived in 2010 alone as a consequence of the *dzud*—bitter winter conditions—which saw temperatures falling as low as –50°C and thick snow burying the grass which resulted in the death of almost 10 million cattle, sheep, goats, horses, yaks and camels (a fifth of the country's total) at a cost of US$398 million. This has further contributed to the challenging fact that a third of citizens live below the poverty line of about US$80 per month. But more than this, it has hurt the herding community's way of life, as nomadism for them is identified with the very spirit of the country (Branigan 2010).

This shift in people and economy has influenced the transition from a centralised to a decentralised system of urban governance. Ulaanbaatar is an independent municipality, governed by a city council. And the city proactively seeks out the exchange of urban planning experiences and good governance—a demonstration of which is Ulaanbaatar's involvement in the ground-breaking UN Global Compact Cities Programme.

Established in 2002, the Global Compact Cities Programme is the urban component of the United Nations Global Compact initiative. It works by practically applying to local government the ten overarching principles of the UN Global Compact—in the domains of human rights, labour, the environment and anti-corruption—which are derived from a set of international declarations including:

- The Universal Declaration of Human Rights

- The International Labour Organisation's Declaration on Fundamental Principles and Rights at Work

- The Rio Declaration on Environment and Development

- The United Nations Convention against Corruption

In addition to the City of Ulaanbaatar, other leading member cities of the UN Global Compact Cities Programme include: City of Asker (Norway), City of As-Salt (Jordan), City of Berlin (Germany), City of Jamshedpur (India), City of Jinan (China), City of Le Havre (France), City of Milwaukee (USA), City of Porto Alegre (Brazil), City of Płock (Poland), City of San Francisco (USA), City of Tshwane (South Africa) and City of Melbourne (Australia). The Global Compact Cities Programme's international secretariat is located at RMIT University in Melbourne, Australia, under the auspices of the UN Global Compact Office in New York.

A key element of Ulaanbaatar's project is clarification of the city's development vision through a participatory process, in order to formulate development strategies and action plans to realise this vision. The desired outcomes include: building institutional capacity for improved governance; establishing frameworks to build an enabling environment for social improvement and economic growth; and providing mechanisms for job creation and sustainable livelihoods.

'Ulaanbaatar's aspiration to learn the harsh lessons from other countries' failed slum re-settlements is really admirable—local consultation and capacity building is key to success in developing Mongolia's capital city', says Professor Paul James, Director of the

UN Global Compact Cities Programme in relation to Ulaanbaatar's membership.

> In 2003 the Mongolian Association of Urban Centres was set up and we have worked with Ulaanbaatar to help establish a 'critical reference group'. This collaboration includes the Mayor's office, local council and NGOs as well as other international partners such as UN-Habitat and Cities Alliance, with the aim of collaboratively developing a planning framework to guide improvements on priority actions such as housing quality, waste management, transport and public safety. An important element of this is to clearly set out the roles and responsibilities of the council, private developers and others.

Work by Ulaanbaatar to date has been productive but difficult because of the ongoing challenge of using a consultative approach to agree the precise process for implementation of this new framework for taking action (such as local training to build capacity). The learning from other more advanced programme participants such as the City of Porto Alegre in Brazil is cited as a quality benchmark here. Professor James concludes:

> Porto Alegre is an impressive and replicable model of how urban development strategies should deal with slums. The starting premise by the Brazilian council here is that it is better to refurbish and reclaim these areas in consultation with the local communities. Demolishing areas and displacing people without a very good reason (such as location or security) is a bad idea as you may just be moving the problem elsewhere and this is both a waste of money and causes social unrest. Our work with Porto Alegre's Chocolatão slum since 2003 has been highly successful as the new suburbs that have been created are self-managed and the benefits are shared. For example, following local consultation on future livelihoods attended by residents, planners and architects alike, a series of purpose-built houses and recycling facilities were constructed with the latter employing local people and the profit from which is shared with residents. This is not about spend-

ing more money, but making the most of the money you
have through long-term, participatory urban planning.

For further information visit:
- www.citycouncil.mn
- www.citiesprogramme.org

(accessed 15 September 2010)

Next, our attention will be aimed at approaches to adapt to climate
change through land-use planning and sustainable building controls
(the definition of adaptation is detailed in Box 9.1).

BOX 9.1 **Adaptation and mitigation**

By 'adaptation' we mean ensuring in the near future your communities are able to live, rest and play in a safe and secure environment.
By contrast, 'mitigation' means reducing CO_2 emissions.

The UN Intergovernmental Panel on Climate Change (IPCC)
highlights the emerging consensus that we have less than five years
to seriously reduce carbon emissions before potentially irrevers-
ible changes to the climate begin to happen should temperatures
rise beyond 2°C (DECC 2009). If these harmful emissions are not
stopped, a future of uncontrolled climate change could mean flooding, heatwaves and unpredictable weather, creating upheaval across
the world. The results of this will include effects on the systems on
which we all depend (such as food growth and energy supplies)
and adverse impacts on human health, housing and livelihoods.

The *Stern Review* (2006) concluded that the economic cost of
tackling climate change could amount to around 1% of world GDP,
but that the costs of not acting could be much higher and equivalent
to 5–20% of GDP now and forever (as a result of declining food
production, loss of infrastructure due to sea-level rise and extreme
weather events and impacts on biodiversity). This startling reality
is reflected in refreshed international efforts to attempt to get all
nations to agree on collective action as captured under the Copenhagen Accord (UNFCCC 2010). Consequently, we need to both
adapt and mitigate when it comes to climate change.

While the exact approach to land-use planning may vary from council to council according to national law and practice, physical development and regeneration in a council area, it is generally governed by strategies and policies contained in a single, overarching development framework. It is best practice for councils to produce this following a period of consultation with interested local stakeholders and sits alongside a planning approval system decreed from national government.

Such a framework may stipulate:

- Percentage of renewable energy in new developments

- Standards of sustainable construction of buildings (you will recall that standards such as LEED and BREEAM were referred to in Chapter 8 in respect of estates management)

- Requirements to undertake a sustainability assessment for major developments (for instance, refer back to the case study from the City of Ekurhuleni in Chapter 7)

- Special zoning arrangement to promote one type of development or exclude another, such as demarcating high-risk flood areas

So, while councils still need to reduce area-based carbon emissions, you must at the same time prepare for the effects of changes to your climate, such as more severe weather events including flooding, bush-fires and so on. This way your council will be best placed to continue to serve its communities.

In many councils such work will already be under way, shaped by local necessity or national planning requirements, as evidenced again by the work of Ekurhuleni and Nillumbik. Others, however, might be just starting out. Either way, a generic approach for the phased preparations of robust adaptation plans is essential (as illustrated below).

[#66] Phased adaptation

Phase 1	Phase 2	Phase 3	Phase 4
• Public commitment to act by council CEO • Baseline impact assessment of issues and risks for council services • Cross-departmental project board established to oversee delivery (i.e. estates management, health)	• Comprehensive risk-based assessment across every council service (e.g. social housing to childcare) • Prioritised action in urgent areas (e.g. emergency planning in relation to flood zones or drought hot spots)	• Comprehensive action plan for all priority areas (e.g. revision of planning guidance on sustainability buildings obligations) • Messaging on actions cascaded to stakeholders by council's leadership (e.g. police, fire service and chambers of commerce)	• Implementation, monitoring and continuous review (via cross-departmental project board) • Alignment with corporate strategy (e.g. no planning approval for building in flood zone) • Ongoing communications on performance to key stakeholders

Source: Based on Defra 2010

Further to this, in the matrix below we move to the next level of detail by taking a particular council service to illustrate what a baseline assessment might look like for each area of activity under a particular theme. For this example we have chosen public healthcare, assuming delivery in Western Europe within a moderate local climate.

Council service	Potential impact of climate change on this service	Possible council responses
Public health	• Higher risk of skin cancer/sunburn owing to hotter summers and increased outdoor recreation	• Consider ways to increase awareness of dangers of exposure and provide more shade in public recreational areas
	• Increased risk of hay fever because of longer growing season	• Ensure antihistamines are available to all who need them

Council service	Potential impact of climate change on this service	Possible council responses
Public health	• Higher temperatures likely to cause increased numbers of insects, in turn giving a higher risk of disease spreading	• Awareness raising for tropical diseases and dehydration
	• Heat stress to the old, poor and vulnerable communities	• Ensure adequate shade and cooling available and local grants available to priority groups for home improvements to ensure they are fit for purpose
	• Higher temperatures likely to increase cases of food poisoning	• Consider ways to increase awareness of food hygiene practices and revisit best practice
	• Higher levels of dust in the air owing to drier summers	• May need to hose down streets in urban areas

As can be seen from the phased adaptation illustrated above, phases 1–3 only require council officer time yet again. However, it is possible that substantial capital investment will be required between phases 3 and 4 to the tune of millions if not billions of dollars, depending on particular circumstances, thus necessitating national government intervention. While numbers of this magnitude are beyond the scope of this book, we do offer insights about cash-generating planning protocols which may contribute towards council funding on this and related sustainability actions; see, for instance, the 'carbon compensation levy' below.

Now, turning to building controls and stipulations, learning from other councils suggests there is an opportunity here to secure a new income stream to subsidise sustainability investments elsewhere (see also intelligent finance in Chapter 8).

[#22] Carbon compensation levy in Milton Keynes, UK

In parts of Milton Keynes developers pay a levy to compensate for the carbon emissions from the use of new properties (Forum for the Future 2010). Monies are collected into a council fund which is spent on local schemes such as insulating older homes which are much less energy-efficient. This is successful for two reasons. First, it is cheaper to save carbon in older homes than make new homes carbon-neutral, and second it raises new capital from the developers for these retrofits. (Note, here, 'compensation' does not equate to an official 'offset' as referred to in Chapter 6.)

The Milton Keynes example is interesting as it raises questions about how best to make use of interventionist planning policies; instead of requiring the developer to produce a percentage of renewable energy from micro-renewables on-site, as is usual in the UK, the council here has concluded that this limited resource is best spent dealing with 'low-hanging fruit' arising from energy-inefficient properties elsewhere.

This model is very much in keeping with the energy management hierarchy which prioritises easy wins; however, there may be even better ways to stretch this limited resource. You will recall for instance in Chapter 8 that reference was made to district heating schemes, and so it may be wise for such levies to be more general in the types of scheme they fund in order that the council is not wedded to any particular resulting spend criteria. That is, the levy is used only to support pre-planned major energy developments, in order to better realise economies of scale and impact.

9.2 Low-carbon trade zones

Most if not all local authorities will have responsibilities for attracting inward investment and supporting the maintenance and creation of jobs as well as the up-skilling of a workforce. Zoning arrangements is one tool at your disposal to assist with this.

Economic zoning powers may or may not be included within the planning function of your council, but there are clearly a number of options to demarcate special areas for low-carbon inward investment. And in terms of the 'upside' of climate change, the opportunities here are enormous, as we see in the example of UAE's Masdar City in Box 9.2.

BOX 9.2 **Climate competitiveness in Masdar City, UAE**

According to world-renowned think-tank AccountAbility and the UN Environment Programme (2010), companies and regions are fighting to win a share of the new low-carbon markets, a sector valued at US$200 billion in 2010.

'A green economy brings with it not only the opportunity to reduce greenhouse gas emissions, but also to generate jobs', concludes UNEP's Executive Director, Achim Steiner.

Low-carbon street lighting is a good example of ferocious competition for the best LED technologies, with Hong Kong, Tianjin and Toronto all vying for the US$1 billion market. (You will recall from Chapter 8 that artificial lighting accounts for about 13% of council energy bills.) Taking this several steps further, the United Arab Emirates is building an entire low-carbon city in Abu Dhabi: Masdar City will combine high-performance architecture with clean fuel sources and aim to attract and retain clean technology industries.

But what does this mean for your council, in terms of the cost-neutral but high-impact actions you can take? While there are multiple possible interventions for planning in relation to economic zoning, one obvious choice is for energy-saving regulations as seen in China's Baoding municipality.

[#23] Special economic zoning in Baoding, China

Baoding, near Beijing in China, has been identified as a low-carbon trade zone and industries are being transformed from heavy manufacturing to low-carbon sectors (AccountAbility and UNEP 2010). The municipality introduced an industrial energy-saving policy and regulations for businesses which was complemented

by financial incentives for solar panel and wind turbine production. Baoding now has 20,000 people working in clean energy.

Elsewhere, the Indian Ministry of Commerce has led the development of green guidelines for special economic zones to attract
foreign direct investment. The draft guidelines focus on the energy
efficiency of new and existing buildings and, if adopted, will lead
to the certification of individual buildings to attract prospective
businesses who want to locate in areas with a low-carbon infrastructure (e.g. reduced costs of estates management).

Similarly, in the UK, a handful of regions have been designated
low-carbon economic areas since 2009, including the Manchester
City Region as an area for the built environment (NWDA 2009). A
five-year retrofit programme will improve the insulation of thousands of homes and offices in Greater Manchester, with small-
scale renewable energy technologies installed and smart meters
introduced so residents can see how much energy they use. In
addition, a 'low-carbon laboratory' will also be established focusing on the research strengths of universities around Manchester
where new innovative technologies will be developed and tested.
One of the most innovative areas of work will be the development
of new finance initiatives such as mortgage products linked to carbon savings. The low-carbon economic area is expected to save
6 million tonnes of carbon, create an additional US$975 million in
the economy and support 34,800 jobs.

So, in practical terms, what can you do to consider area-based
options for designation of low-carbon trade zones? Such a zone may
be best targeted at a particular type of technology based on either
your local specialism or natural environment (e.g. biomass or wave)
or it may be more generic. The key point is that you are marketing
your authority as encouraging and 'open for business' in the clean
technology industry.

Another incisive intervention a council may wish to make is in connection to developing the next generation of skilled clean technology
workers.

[#67] Apprenticeships for a near future

Many if not all local authorities will already be investing in youth training or back-to-work schemes for the unemployed, in association with local education institutions and the local chamber of commerce.

How then are you apportioning part of this existing budget to 'near future' apprenticeships in terms of the next generation of trainees? In what way are you partnering with business leaders to equip the local workforce with the appropriate skills and expertise to participate in the clean technology industry?

According to your particular assets, needs and vulnerable areas in the local labour market, this may be targeted for school leavers or the long-term unemployed in more deprived areas, and could be tailored around a specific technology (such as wind or hydropower).

A fundamentally important element of this is that local people benefit from this new development, either directly through training or employment, or indirectly via additional monies spent locally on goods and services. Again, keeping money local is imperative for the intervention to be desirable.

Working with business to train up new generations of clean technology employees leads nicely on to other ways for you to work with business partners.

9.3 Business incubation, signals and controls

As with skills development above, it is probable that your council has a dedicated person or team looking to nurture start-up companies so they mature and grow in a healthy fashion. Crucial, however, is that people designated with business start-up roles are not left to struggle with this alone, and instead are working with colleagues across the council to identify sustainability-related commercial opportunities. By working together in this way your council has an enormous role to play in enabling winning companies to succeed. This can be delivered in a number of ways.

[#68, #69, #70] Clean-tech business clubs, clear market signals and single contact point

Providing forums for like-minded firms and other potential commercial partners to come together to network and develop opportunities to work together is important. This can take the form of an informal environmental business club or more formal sector clusters which you could facilitate either with staff time or by providing a regular place to meet at your council offices.

An example of this, Invest in Finland (AccountAbility and UNEP), set up a clean technology cluster to provide networking opportunities on venture capital for companies, investors, academics and others which has helped create 20 high-growth companies annually. As a result 10% of all inward investment in 2009 was in clean tech.

At the same time, clean technology companies may simply want a clear signal from the council that it is serious about investing in the clean-tech industry. Policy planning guidelines will assist here, such as what type of renewable or clean technology is preferred by the council and where the council wishes this technology to be sited. In addition, this needs to be backed up by a clear communications strategy for cascading the message to businesses and consideration that some firms may need to have their hand held while they navigate the sometimes complex world of local planning law! Brazil, for instance, has been offering legal support for the development of wind, biomass and hydro schemes since 2002. This is expected to have helped create 150,000 jobs and attract US$2.6 billion in investment.

What does this mean in practice for your local authority? Perhaps it is about identifying a small group of clean technology companies who you then approach to support or are derived from a sub-group of an existing business club. Alongside this, you could nominate a dedicated single point of contact at the council who can deal with or refer any requests for support or planning clarity (this will avoid a company's confusion and frustration if forced to deal with multiple persons across the council ranging from business development to planning to environmental health departments).

And again, remember: all that this requires is council staff time, so it comes down to the issue of reprioritising and deciding to support tomorrow's business leaders in your authority.

In addition to putting in place these *enablers*, it may also be appropriate for your council to instil some *controls* as part of building your reputation as a 'location of choice' for low-carbon investment. An example of this in practice is cases from the Japanese cities Kyoto and Tokyo.

[#24] **Mandatory carbon reductions for companies in Kyoto and Tokyo, Japan**

Local councils in Japan have the authority to take legislative action when the national government itself has not enacted specific policies and measures towards climate change (LGA 2009). As a result some have mandated certain industries to formulate CO_2 reduction plans, among other measures such as local emissions trading and the buying of renewable energy bonds.

For instance, Tokyo Metropolitan requires companies to formulate emission reduction plans and for retailers to place energy performance labels on electrical equipment. Similarly, the City of Kyoto requires businesses to formulate and periodically report on progress towards GHG reduction plans.

Having considered how to engage your businesses, let us now turn attention to the overlooked role of green spaces.

9.4 **Green spaces infrastructure**

'Green spaces' is the catch-all term for urban parks and natural play areas, woodlands, local wildlife sites and nature reserves, allotments

Did you know?

Green spaces have an economic value beyond leisure and
health benefits: they also contribute to community cohesion by
bringing together different people of all ages and groups, and
help to tackle climate change by acting as an urban coolant and
flood defence.

and community gardens and other open spaces. So when we talk about 'green space infrastructure' it means joining up these areas to create green facilities or a corridor which is more than the mere sum of its parts.

Over the past several years thinking and practice on such green space has moved on from ecology to economics (Natural England 2009) which recognises the role green spaces play in contributing to tourism, health and well-being and mitigation of climate change as well as leisure, as illustrated in the tip below.

[#71] **The value of green spaces**

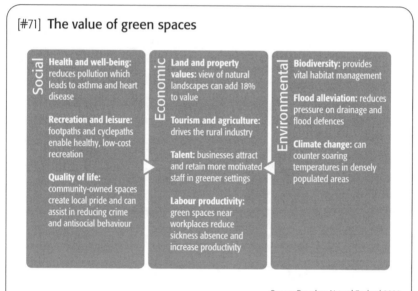

Source: Based on Natural England 2009

So, it is in your interests to ensure that your council keeps apace with the latest thinking on the value of green space accordingly. In practice this means formulating a green space strategy with colleagues from across planning, environment, health, leisure and crime departments. By pooling know-how and existing resources the council will be better placed to deliver on mutually supportive goals and do more with less.

However, not only are green spaces important for these key social, economic and environmental reasons, they are also a valuable tool in mobilising residents to get involved with and take ownership of these community assets (e.g. maintenance and enhancement) as seen in Uganda.

[#25] Growling gardeners in Kampala, Uganda

As a council, you will most likely already have a database of ready, willing and able conservation volunteers who assist with anything from repairing footpaths to thinning woodland, and this is a very valuable (and free) contribution. One of the problems with this approach, however, is that there is one limiting factor to scaling up their impact. You! Think about how well this 'labour bank' could be used if you gave permission for local residents to become 'growling gardeners'. (They growl because they dislike unused and unloved green spaces and are passionate about improving them!)

Take the excellent learning from Kampala, the capital city of Uganda, where 'problematic' unofficial urban farms were embraced by a new urban growing policy which revolutionised the local food system and surrounding green spaces (Grist 2007).

So, as a self-managed group, conservation enthusiasts similar to those in Uganda could work on anything from urban bee-keeping, reclaiming unwanted small plots of land as community allotments, to creating bird nest boxes or ponds in local woodlands, to establishing community roof or wall gardens.

This could be piloted in clearly defined areas and supported by council officers through training and mentoring, as well as practical guidance on any environmental health risks. Local community groups could be set up alongside this to fundraise for any equipment or licence fees needed, or consider that a one-off start-up cost would be more than offset by the reduction in external contractor costs from similar work.

The result would be a cost-neutral enhancement in the economic value of your council's green spaces. Simple but powerful stuff!

Having now reviewed the role of economic development and planning, in the next chapter we switch attention to how waste and environmental services can support your drive to sustainability.

Key learning

✓ Economic development and planning raise both tremendous opportunities and risks for sustainability, ranging from creating new employment to increasing pollution.

✓ A phased approach to climate adaptation is vital for future-proofing your council against dramatic changes in the weather, which requires cross-departmental working to devise contingency plans for each of your key services.

✓ Special economic zoning can help stimulate your ability to attract inward investment for clean technology development.

✓ Working with businesses may involve helping them to navigate local planning or legal barriers, but also laying down performance protocols on sustainability.

✓ You should fully understand the economic value of your green infrastructure, as it attracts talent and supports the tourism industry as well as having a positive impact on residents' health and well-being.

10

Waste and environmental services

What makes me uncomfortable is that we are feeding so much fish protein to pets when there isn't enough fish in the world to give everyone a healthy of amount of fish in their diet (Callum Roberts, Professor of Marine Conservation, University of York, 2010, responding to news that pet food is to be sold using certified sustainable fish).

Typical sustainability actions and outcomes	Cost-neutral interventions
10.1 The asset at the bottom of your residents' bins	#72
10.2 Reduction	#26, #73, #74, #75, #76, #77
10.3 Repair or re-use	#78, #27
10.4 Recycling	#6, #28, #79, #80, #29

10.1 **The asset at the bottom of your residents' bins**

Taking action on waste is essential for councils. As we saw earlier in the book in terms of lifestyles and population growth, humankind consumes natural resources at an unsustainable rate and contributes unnecessarily to climate change. Each year we generate billions of tonnes of waste from households, government and industry with the majority of this ending up in landfill, where biodegradable waste generates methane, a powerful greenhouse gas. In addition, much valuable energy is used up in making new products to feed consumer lifestyles which are later disposed of; this also contributes to climate change.

An illustration of waste arising from economic activity is shown in Figure 10.1.1, followed by a focus on household waste. Figure 10.1.1 takes the UK as an example, although clearly waste profiles will differ from council to council according to industry bias, affluence and consumer attitudes.

So what type of waste would we find in our residents' bins? Again, this will vary from country to country, but a likely composition taken from the UK is illustrated in Figure 10.1.2. Here we can see that, all things being equal in terms of return on one's efforts, priority should be given to garden waste, paper and cardboard, and kitchen waste.

FIGURE 10.1.1 **Waste arising by economic activity**

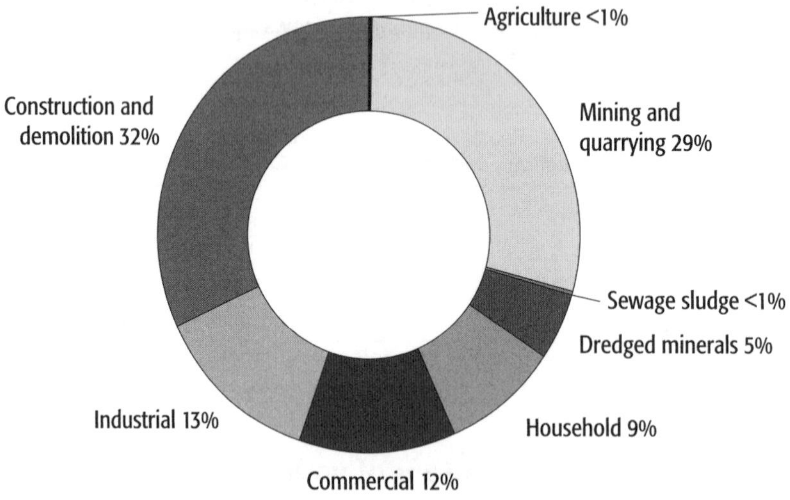

Agriculture <1%

Construction and demolition 32%

Mining and quarrying 29%

Sewage sludge <1%

Dredged minerals 5%

Industrial 13%

Household 9%

Commercial 12%

Source: Parfitt 2002

The apparent 'minor' 9% contribution made by municipal waste (Fig. 10.1.1) needs to be taken with caution. For instance, levels of waste arising from commercial and industrial waste owes much to the fact that companies produce products and packaging which will be consumed by your residents and most likely end up in a council refuse bin.

FIGURE 10.1.2 **Composition of household waste**

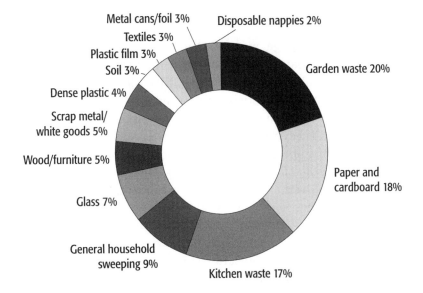

Source: Parfitt 2002

However, although we have seen that prioritisation against domestic waste profiles would be beneficial, there are other influences to consider:

- A council's technical ability to process certain types of waste (e.g. trying to recycle elements of the general household waste sweepings)

- The logistical cost of transporting heavy and loosely presented waste (e.g. garden waste is mostly grass cuttings made of water)

- Residents' willingness to take action on certain types of waste (e.g. kitchen waste may be seen as 'smelly and messy' to handle)

- The volatility of the sales markets for recycled materials such as metals or textiles (which means a council may or may not offset some of the costs for its waste collection service)

At the same time, though, we need to understand that different councils will of course have different duties and powers related to waste and environmental services. For some, this will solely relate to an obligation to collect domestic waste for disposal, while, at the other end of the spectrum, an authority may have responsibilities for waste minimisation and recycling for both domestic and business customers. In addition, some councils will be facing an annual increase in statutory targets and financial penalties as well as 'naming and shaming' by national government for failures to comply.

Our primary focus here, then, as always, is to look at interventions you can make given your particular contexts which improve sustainability while being cost-neutral. As such we will hone in on the latest thinking in terms of waste reduction for re-use and recycling only and we will also confine this to domestic waste (noting that we touched on the council's own waste from estates in Chapter 8 and that we will work on the assumption that business waste is a separate for-fee service). Additionally, we will also omit incineration or energy-from-waste considerations (such as anaerobic digestion) for reasons of high cost investment and long payback periods as they are beyond the scope of this book.

Given all of this, your approach to selecting interventions should be guided by the 'universally accepted' waste hierarchy, as depicted in Figure 10.1.3. Put simply, this means you reduce the waste arising in the first place, before looking at options to repair or re-use any waste, before recycling other waste, and finally, only then considering incineration or landfill disposal for any remaining waste.

FIGURE 10.1.3 **Waste hierarchy**

In saying this, we should note that some of the latest environmental research suggests that, while overall recycling remains the preferred option compared with incineration, it is not always the case, as suggested next.

[#72] **Recycling as the most effective disposal method (kind of)**

According to a report by WRAP on behalf of the UK Government, recycling is almost always the best way to get rid of waste (*The Environmentalist* 2010). The report, which addresses persistent claims that householders are often wasting their time recycling, calls for better recycling facilities as well as, intriguingly, an increase in incineration of waste.

WRAP analysed different materials measured by four criteria: energy use, water, other resource use and greenhouse gas emissions. It found, for biopolymers, the preferable option is recycling; for textiles, re-use is optimal; for food and garden waste, anaerobic digestion looks preferable; for wood and plastics, recycling is the best option because recycling has improved; and for paper and cardboard, it depends on the quality of the material: the higher the quality, the better it is to recycle, but as you go down to the lower end, energy recovery by incineration may be preferable. The study also considered the impact of transporting waste to other countries—often to China—for recycling. It found that overseas transport was still better than sending it to landfill.

The take-out for your council is to be very clear on what the criteria are for selecting a particular waste disposal method. The investment you will be making here in the first instance to research the options is staff only. So, your course of action may again be constrained by the availability and quality of certain recycling or incineration technologies in your particular country compared with the UK. Or perhaps your criteria are different from the WRAP study: for instance, if we added social criteria, too, it could be argued it was unethical to 'dump' one nation's waste on the doorstep of another.

In short, we all have assets at the bottom of our refuse bin. We often throw away materials that we or our neighbours could use and gain value from. And every time we do throw things away this increases the burden on our local taxes (in terms of landfill disposal costs), so we are moving in ever-decreasing circles!

10.2 **Reduction**

In alignment with the waste hierarchy we begin then by looking at zero-cost schemes to reduce waste. First, it is proposed you work back through your residents' 'consumption chain', spending time to engage with the companies who manufacture, package and sell most of the products your residents use.

Have you ever thought about asking or demanding that companies 'up their game'? Here are a few ideas about what you might want to do directly or support through your community messaging campaigns, depending on your powers and appetite! Examples of how this might work in practice are shared below, starting with plastic bags in San Francisco.

[#26, #73, #74] Swimming upstream with retailers in San Francisco, USA; eradicating packaging from the schools menu in Germany; junking the junk mail in the UK

Sacking the sacks: San Francisco became the first US city to pass a ban on non-recyclable plastic bags at major supermarkets (Grist 2007). Stores that hand out about 180 million plastic bags a year must use compostable, recyclable ones made from potato starch or revert to recyclable paper. Similar bans are in place in South Africa, Taiwan, Bangladesh and Paris.

Taking waste off the menu: Under the auspices of the Foundation for Environmental Education (the European eco-schools initiative), educators in Germany are de-selecting food products from their school menus that have comparatively high packaging content.[3]

Junking the junk mail: In the UK, all residents can opt out of receiving junk mail by registering online with the Royal Mail.[4] Knowsley Council in Merseyside, UK, visits all households in the authority to make residents aware of this option as part of a wider door-to-door behaviour change campaign.

Second, further downstream, let us now turn to what councils can do to support and encourage responsible consumers, for instance, in relation to food and festive presents.

[#75, #76] Food for thought, and celebrating festive reductions

By planning grocery shopping better, your residents can cut down on unnecessary kitchen waste which will help out with their household bills and budgets. Approximately one-third of food bought by UK households can end up in the bin (*The Environmentalist* 2010). A way to correct this is to ask households to log all food that they throw away over a one-month period, to review the results, do a stock-take and think again about the right amounts of each food product they actually need. And remember: always go by the 'use by' date and not the 'sell by' date for when you do eventually decide to dispose of any food waste.

Another simple but powerful way to get the message home on waste reduction is awareness campaigns around major festive periods, such as Christmas, Diwali, Eid, Thanksgiving, Yom Kippur and other religious or national holidays. For instance, do you really need to wrap up all your Christmas presents? Can we select a chocolate Easter egg that is stand-alone and not in lots of unnecessary packaging? All of which is likely to save families money at an already expensive time of the year!

3 Eco-schools, www.eco-schools.org, accessed April 2010.
4 Royal Mail, www.royalmail.com, accessed April 2010.

Speaking through existing platforms such as community news-letters or school and neighbourhood events, council officers will be able to share locally relevant, 'top ten' handy hints from the above. It is critical that this complements any national campaigns, if any, to avoid confusing and conflicting public messages.

In closing this section we come to perhaps one of the more controversial tips in this book—pets—which warrants a specific analysis in its own right!

[#77] **Can you be a responsible citizen and have a pet?**

As indicated by the quote from Professor Roberts at the University of York that introduces this chapter (Vaughan 2010), there is an increasing body of evidence that household pets are just as bad news for the planet as cars, population growth and other ticking time bombs. Not only in terms of the availability of food to feed the poor but also the waste arising and the carbon footprint of domestic animals.

San Francisco estimates that up to 5% of all landfill waste now arises from pet waste and the author of a provocative new book claims that the energy required to feed a cat is the same as that needed to build and drive a VW Golf 6,000 miles a year (Vale 2009). Vale says that chicken, turkey or rabbit has a lower impact than red meat or fish when used as pet food.

Given the startling statistics, practical actions councils can take are to refine communications with residents and educators alike, so people understand the full implications of their domestic choices (whether buying a new house or car, or deciding to have more children or a pet). Trade-offs are required here; by helping residents to understand the true extent of their footprint they will be better placed to make an informed, positive choice on sustainability matters.

10.3 **Repair or re-use**

We move on now to look at some novel ideas on cost-neutral ways to mend or re-use goods, within your communities.

[#78] **Low-tech community swap shops**

The online re-using revolution instigated by Freecycle and other similar initiatives should be welcomed and applauded as a way for residents to re-use unwanted items. However, not everyone is able do things online, either because they do not have access to a computer or through a lack of IT literacy. Or, perhaps, they just prefer doing things face-to-face with friends and family from their community.

Consequently, there has been a spike of interest among councils about 'low-tech' alternatives to Freecycle. Put simply, a 'community swap shop' is a group of people who know each other coming together every few months. Likely participants to this would be homemakers and young children, interested in swapping shoes, toys and other equipment which becomes unnecessary as tastes change or a child grows.

Goods can be new but unwanted, old but in good shape or a bit worn and just need repair.

And note these fun events are also great for community cohesion, by providing an opportunity to meet some of your neighbours for the first time or to get to know them better! The gatherings could also be used as a method to promote your other sustainability initiatives.

Maybe this is something your council can suggest and support to interested people, perhaps by hosting one as a pilot at a council site or park (which would further encourage use of the community facility).

Next, we return to engaging retailers, this time an anecdote on re-usable items from Barnsley in the UK.

[#27] **Conditioning shoppers to re-use fabric conditioner in Barnsley, UK**

Barnsley Council has been successfully participating in a trial with Asda stores (part of the Wal-Mart chain) on a re-usable fabric conditioner product (Serventi 2010).

Using a self-dispensing technology, fabric conditioner is piped to re-usable containers at a dispensing point in the retail aisle from the back of the store via overhead pipes. It allows customers to purchase concentrated fabric conditioner in re-usable pouches that can be refilled up to 10 times, saving approximately US$1 each time compared with the same volume of product in traditional plastic bottles.

As well as offering consumer savings, the new technology offers retailers significant business benefits including carbon impact reduction across the entire supply chain. It also has the potential to free up in-store sales space and offer transportation and storage cost savings.

So, how about speaking to one of the major retailers in your local area to see what the scope is for a similar pilot in your area?

10.4 **Recycling**

Finally, we turn our attention to recycling. Again, your scope for cost-neutral interventions here will depend on particular circumstances in terms of powers, duties and available technologies (recognising that recycling facilities can involve multi-million dollar investments).

You will recall, for instance, in Chapter 8 we looked at the whole-life costing example from Wakefield Council that calculated it was, on balance, better value for money to use recycled kerb materials for its road network rather than traditional materials.

So, working on the assumption that you do recycle, we propose some more ideas here. But first we set the scene with a case study from Krakow in Poland.

[#6] **Festival of recycling: Municipality of Krakow, Poland**

Krakow is ranked as the fourth largest industrial city in the country, with metallurgic, tobacco and pharmaceutical industries dominating. The local labour market benefits from the fact that the city metropolitan area with its cultural history is an attractive place to live, with approximately 1.5 million residents, many of whom are highly qualified. This is reflected in the fact that the unemployment rate in Krakow is one of the lowest in Poland.

Driving forward on sustainability performance is one part of Krakow's aspiration to be a world-leading city. Consequently, the council has prioritised a number of key issues such as public transport, waste water and waste management.

'Our key success is the practical programme of delivery for these current priorities, and "future-proofing" for tomorrows dilemmas', says Wiesław Starowicz, Deputy Mayor of Krakow.

The highlights for Starowicz are the tangible improvements to green spaces, water quality, noise pollution, energy from waste incineration, and greenhouse gas emissions. While at the same time pointing to the fact that the new waste water treatment facility is operating at 50% capacity in the expectation that, as the city develops, the council's environmental management obligations might also. Starowicz continues:

> A current challenge we are dealing with at the moment is that while environmental awareness among the residents of Krakow is high, environmental behaviour has been comparatively weak. So we have had to be creative to raise interest and change attitudes—such as through the popular Festival of Recycling.

With regard to waste collection and segregation, the council ambitiously believes it is catching up with the richest countries in the world; however, at present the council only recovers a small percentage of waste and admits it still has a lot to learn in this area. This is why for the last few years the city has been organising the largest education event in Poland, promoting the idea of recycling—the Festival of Recycling. In this non-banal way the council wants to show residents that the environment and recycling are not an abstract notion, isolated from everyday life.

The most spectacular part of each Festival is the unveiling of an installation built from recyclable waste. Up to now, they have built the Krakow Barbican out of 60,000 aluminium cans, and Sukiennice—the historic Krakow Cloth Hall—out of 40,000 glass bottles, among others. The idea here is to capture people's imagination first and then focus attention on the sheer scale of unnecessary waste.

The Festival comprises a dozen or so diverse concerts, special attractions for children, conferences and seminars, which show that recycling need not be either boring or a hard subject.

Crucially, a constant element of the Festival is collection of recyclable waste from residents. In return, the inhabitants get plant seedlings and other small gifts. The people of Krakow have been bringing more waste to the event year-on-year, one indicator of success.

A key factor in this and other achievements on sustainability has been long and hard efforts to get support from various partners to build consensus: for instance, wider work on the European Week of Sustainable Transport. This has included car-free days, a mobility forum devoted to cycling meetings and cleaner air.

The Festival is deemed cost-neutral by the council as it diverts waste from landfill and is also supported by a national policy instrument whereby all funds collected from environmental charges are spent on environmental improvement activities.

This fund is vital to ongoing sustainability work at the council as it accounts for 1% of the total budget, and will remain so for the foreseeable future. This is ever more important given that the wider budget has decreased by 10% during the economic downturn, which, while not as severe as in some parts of Europe and the USA, is still a challenging situation.

Did you know?

Many schools are turning to waste wood as an on-site, alternative source of fuel, both to reduce their dependency on harmful fossil fuels but also to show children how these new technologies work in practice.

Now that we have seen the importance of recycling as a route to stimulate public interest, we will look at another simple way of engaging residents—composting—beginning with an example from Ecuador.

[#28, #79] **Composting galore in Bahía de Caráquez, Ecuador; and making your own home composter**

Composting is a fantastic way to divert waste from landfill and deliver a 'social dividend' at the same time such as its contribution to community gardening or alleviating underdeveloped sanitation.

Bahía de Caráquez declared itself an ecological city in the late 1990s following the implementation of a strategy to recover from severe natural disasters (Grist 2007). Since that time the council has developed programmes to protect biodiversity and to revegetate and reverse erosion as part of marking itself out as an eco-tourist destination. Further to this, public markets and households in the city voluntarily contribute to community composting and agriculture.

Your residents can make their own basic, home composter too. All it takes is a timber frame from reclaimed wood waste, covered with old carpet or plastic sheeting to retain moisture and heat (Yarrow 2008).

Perhaps more revolutionary is the composting toilet. This low-cost, waterless, odourless toilet is linked to a small composting facility, the by-products of which can be used in agriculture. Pioneered in Sweden, and already in use in the USA and China, this simple but powerful technology may pay for itself in areas where people do not have access to appropriate sanitation facilities (Brown 2009).

So, can councils encourage schools to recycle and compost more? Even if you are already educating school teachers, parents and pupils on these issues is there someone you are missing from the list? The answer to both questions is 'yes'!

[#80] Amending job descriptions of school janitors

A key way to boost school recycling rates is to ensure that the school janitor or building manager is required to recycle and compost. The best way to do this is to ensure it is written into their job descriptions. (You will recall this as a catalytic action recommended under the human resources section of the corporate resources chapter, earlier in the book.) This may mean renegotiating with employees or waiting until vacancies arise. Either way it will be well worth the wait! This 'stick' could be complemented by a 'carrot', perhaps an authority-wide competition whereby schools compete for a prize, which is paid for by the savings made on landfill diversion.

Further to this approach for schools (and building on the themes of encouragement versus enforcement in Chapter 3), it is possible for councils to take this a step further. Rewarding domestic customers for recycling more by offering financial incentives, or indeed, financial penalties for those who do not, is beginning to be introduced by many councils. Others are looking at lowering the frequency of refuse collection compared with that of recyclables: for instance, refuse is only collected fortnightly while recyclables are collected weekly to force people to recycle more. Belgium has taken such a step.

[#29] Pay-as-you-throw in Flanders, Belgium

A council scheme to charge residents extra for throwing out excessive household refuse, with rebates for those who recycle more, has been up and running in Flanders for several years now (Sherman 2007).

A transparent chip is used to identify a bin which is then weighed and loaded on to a wagon, with householders subsequently billed for non-recyclable waste.

Waste is billed at 15 cents per kilogram, equal to US$75 per household per year. Low-waste households disposing of US$30 worth a year have a rebate of US$45. Those disposing of US$120 worth pay an extra US$45. The idea is that this will be cost-neutral once whole-life costing is taken into consideration.

The plan is part of a Flemish waste strategy that demands greater recycling targets for household waste to make big cuts in landfill as, under EU law, councils such as Flanders will have to recycle at least 35% of household waste from 2010 (rising to 50% by 2020).

Given the premise for this book, it is questionable whether such interventions might fail our selection criteria on desirability grounds alone, although this in part will be shaped by the cultural context. So, what is politically acceptable in Belgium may be unacceptable elsewhere, for instance the UK where there has been a media backlash against such schemes. However, it is worth checking out these ideas to determine whether a pilot in your area could be feasible.

Having now completed our assessment of waste, in the next chapter we look at how we can drive down costs and emissions as part of effective fleet management and logistics.

Key learning

✓ Never underestimate the value to you and others of the assets in your residents' waste bins.

✓ Follow the waste hierarchy in your decision-making, starting with reduction before looking at recycling ideas, in order to limit the financial liability for disposal.

✓ Novel ways of working may be open to exploration, such as partnering with retailers to minimise product packaging through to low-tech community swap days.

11
Fleet and logistics

While billions are being spent on having engineers make the car less environmentally harmful, let's be aware: The 'zero carbon vehicle' was invented more than 200 years ago and is called 'bicycle' (Konrad Otto-Zimmermann, Secretary General, ICLEI–Local Governments for Sustainability, 2010).

Typical sustainability actions and outcomes	Cost-neutral interventions
11.1 Driving down emissions and costs	–
11.2 Employee commuting	#30, #81
11.3 Business travel	#82, # 83, #31, #84. #7, #85
11.4 Public travel	#32, #33, #86, #34, #35, #36, #37, #87, #88

11.1 **Driving down emissions and costs**

Transport plays a critical role in how we live, work and play.

For some people effective transportation is simply about the quickest, cheapest or most comfortable means to go from point A to point B. For others, it is an essential aspect of going about their daily job.

For some, in rural areas or who are immobile or feel vulnerable, it is a vital lifeline that connects them to the rest of the world; in such cases it is even psychologically associated with independence and personal freedom.

Yet, as we saw from Figure 9.1, about one-seventh (14%) of all GHG emissions arise from transport. Added to the huge economic loss associated with traffic congestion, which is estimated to cost US$200–1,000 per driver in the USA and equivalent to 1% of GDP in the EU,[5] we begin to see the real cost of our transport decisions.

Consequently, how to enjoy the benefits of travelling while minimising costs as well as the adverse economic and environmental impacts it currently creates is the main challenge for leaders in local government.

In particular, this means looking at modes of transport that are the most damaging, notably the car, as detailed in Figure 11.1 using evidence from the UK.

FIGURE 11.1 **CO_2 emissions by mode of domestic travel**

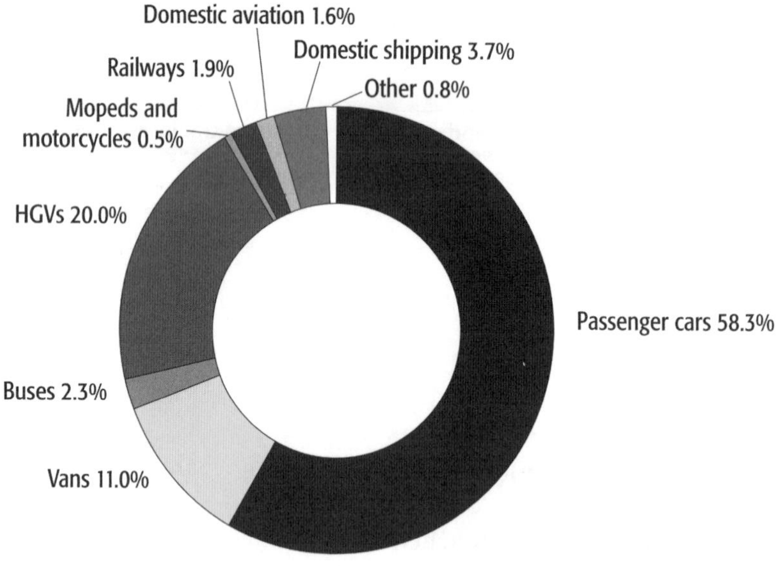

Source: Department for Transport 2009

5 Global Alliance for EcoMobility, ICLEI, www.ecomobility.org, accessed April 2010.

But again, according to country of operation, councils may have different powers and duties (as is the case with planning and waste), and modes of travel and types of journey may also vary depending on geographical spread, standard of living and cultural norms. So, as always, our focus here is on cost-neutral and high-impact interventions that you can make on transport planning appropriate to your local authority.

As with previous decision-making hierarchies (namely, energy and waste) we first look to reducing use before we examine any renewable fuel opportunities.

Given this, the chapter aims to provide you with critical insights across three core areas of work: namely, employee commuting (council officer transport to and from the workplace), business travel (council fleet and officer travel during working hours) and public travel (how a council plans for residents' travel and business logistics). That is, we begin with areas of activity that are in the gift of a council to control and then turn to areas where you can have influence.

This means we only briefly consider major renewable fuel sources for transport as such interventions can have major cost implications, long payback periods and tend to require a lead role from national government and the private sector. As you will see later, we propose that the role for local government in this area is to be a partner of choice, helping to stimulate the market, possibly as a fuel customer or in terms of local integrated transport plans. This planning should also sit alongside wider energy-related considerations, such as the 'smart grid', low-carbon distribution networks we referred to under estates management (in Chapter 8).

11.2 **Employee commuting**

The journey your employees make to and from work at the council can be influenced in a number of ways, ranging from asking people to volunteer to leave their car at home once a week, or for them to work from home, through to setting up car-sharing schemes and making people aware of the alternative options for them such as public transport and cycling. A relevant example is the following actions taken by the City of Gothenburg in Sweden.

[#30] 'Which day do I leave my car at home?' in Gothenburg, Sweden

Following a campaign by the council, 100,000 people were encouraged by their employers to travel to and from work without taking a car during 'Mobility Week'. In total 42 employers in Gothenburg took on a challenge to participate in the initiative. This included the council itself, contributing 45,000 participants.[6]

The aim was to inform and inspire the residents of Gothenburg to actively reflect on their everyday choice of transport and to inspire and motivate other employers to encourage their co-workers in not taking their cars to work.

Employees registered their commitment on a website[7] where each employer or division could set a goal for how many colleagues would sign up. The result was made public afterwards to create a 'competitive' atmosphere between participating companies.

The employees represented close to a third of all those employed in Gothenburg, which has massive impacts on awareness, one of our key aims. Also, the initiative significantly reduced emissions from car journeys during the campaign week and has the potential to do so in the future too as people consider integrating alternatives to driving a car to and from work into their daily lives.

Any similar initiative should primarily generate a good-humoured and lively discussion, which perhaps might then lead to more serious activities, such as the adoption of a sustainable travel incentive and the introduction of a car pool.

Regardless of your particular mix of initiatives in this regard, developing and communicating a staff travel plan is pivotal to success. Motivating factors for staff to participate may include wider reasons such as the health benefits associated with switching from driving to cycling or walking on the one hand or, on the other hand, improvements in local air quality from a reduction in tailpipe fumes. (The

6 Covenant of Mayors, www.eumayors.eu, accessed April 2010.
7 www.nyavagvanor.se, accessed 16 September 2010.

latter will be explored further in the next chapter on community man-agement.)

As part of this, 'carrot and stick' mechanisms to incentivise or penalise should again be explored to effect real and lasting behaviour change, as detailed below.

[#81] **Swiping away the car-parking addicts**

In addition to the incentive approach undertaken in Gothenburg, above, penalties could also be introduced. One example could be offering staff a permit to use the free or subsidised staff car park four days per week. An electronic swipe card system can be used here for monitoring, control and reporting purposes, as is used by Worcester County Council in the UK (Low Carbon Best Practice Exchange 2010). The cost of the card system is at least offset by the reduction in car park maintenance and may lead to consider-able cost savings.

Alternatively, you may wish to remove facilities or any subsidy all together. Either way, there are opportunities for you to save money here! However, this may prove very unpopular in one sin-gle swoop and so perhaps a phased approach starting with the first model of reducing entitlements is more preferable.

The counter-argument to any complaints from staff about these plans is that the current provision or subsidy of car-parking facili-ties is not a fair system anyhow as, in essence, it rewards one form of staff travel over another. That is, if you get a bus or a train or cycle to work, the council is not subsidising the journey, so why should car-parking be subsidised? We need to wean ourselves off this car-centric way of working and this is as good a place to start as any.

We now turn to council staff transport when commuting for busi-ness purposes.

11.3 **Business travel**

As noted from the outset of this chapter, different councils will have different powers and duties related to transport planning, one of which may or may not concern certain stringent vehicle emission standards such as those in force in California, China, the EU and Japan (Feung and Sauer 2004). For instance, the EU New Car CO_2 Regulation requires local authorities to procure a fleet with emissions of no greater than 130 gCO_2/km by 2011 and 95 gCO_2/km by 2020.

This can be one of several important considerations in any whole-life costing (a concept discussed previously under procurement in Chapter 8) in the context of alternative purchasing options within your business fleet. It is vital that all avenues for savings are explored.

With this in mind, what we focus on here are ideas to reduce emissions and costs, regardless of your particular national emissions laws. In particular, we will look at four key areas for positive impact, which are:

- Vehicle replacement

- Choice of fuel

- Use of grey fleet

- Smarter driving

We begin with vehicle replacement.

[#82] **From showroom to end-of-life vehicle recycling**

Whole-life costing to inform your choice of fleet vehicle should, as a minimum, consider carbon, smarter-driver enabling features, and waste (APSE 2009). Each is detailed below.

In terms of carbon, this relates to:

- Engine CO_2 efficiency in terms of gCO_2/km and your national emissions standards

- Compatibility of alternative fuels

- Fuel economy miles per gallon (MPG)

Design-enabling features that assist smarter-driving would include:

- Gear shift indicators

- Tyre pressure monitoring systems

- Air conditioning with low global warming potential (GWP)

- Low-rolling-resistance tyres

- Low-viscosity engine lubricants

Finally, in respect of waste, this would include:

- Retreading tyres

- Repairing windscreens

- Disposal of waste oil

- End-of-life vehicle recycling

So, when preparing to buy, make sure you get some of the answers to these questions from the salesperson you are speaking to!

In looking at the vehicle we also need to consider the appropriate choice of fuel, which forms our next tip.

[#83] **Fuelling ideas for selection**

Carbon dioxide emissions are linked directly to fuel consumption, in that the more fuel a vehicle uses, the more carbon dioxide it emits.

To consider realistic alternatives, we contrast the likely environmental benefits of different fuels compared with petrol in Table 11.3. As is evident, purely on environmental grounds, even a switch to another fossil fuel in the form of diesel has considerable positive benefits. While making use of electric battery vehicles has the added advantage of eradicating other exhaust pipe pollutants such as particulates and NO_x (which contribute to asthma problems and can cause acid rain, respectively) in addition to reducing carbon emissions. At the same time, you also need to be aware of the wider sustainability issues associated with alternative fuel choices: for instance, the source of electricity for battery vehicles may be a fossil-fuel power station or growing biofuels can compete with food crop production and push up food prices for poor people as a result.

With respect to whole-life costing you also need to consider non-environmental considerations, of course. Not just price variations or vehicle retrofit costs, but also the reliability of supply (e.g. refuelling stations for electric batteries) versus benefits (e.g. from tax breaks on fuel duty).

TABLE 11.3 **Emissions comparison by fuel type**

	Petrol	Diesel	Electric	CNG	LPG	Bio-diesel	Bioeth-anol
CO_2 reduction		15–25%	35–40%	10–15%		60%	25%
Other air pollutants			No exhaust	No particulates, 80% lower NO_x			
Wider sustainability			Fossil fuel electricity?			Competition with food crop growing?	

Source: Vaze 2009

Some councils are even experimenting with novel fuel types that involve substances previously considered to be waste, such as in Thailand.

[#31] Transport fuel innovations in Bangkok, Thailand

A five-year green strategy to move the city away from its legacy of smokestacks and smog has included efforts to recycle residents' used cooking oil (Grist 2007). The cooking oil is used to make biodiesel, reducing GHG emissions from vehicles.

An additional advantage is that it diverts waste from landfill, and prevents releases of fats and oils which would damage local water quality.

This leads us to a wider ownership debate on grey fleet.

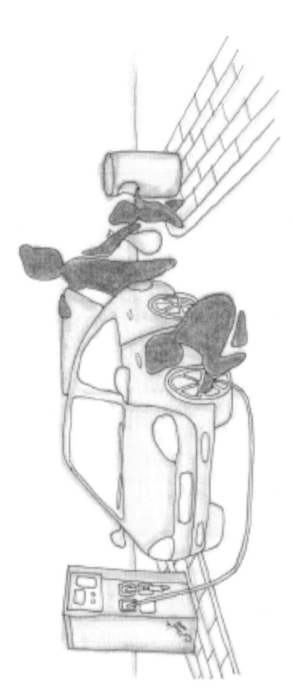

Did you know?

By driving in a smarter way—at home or work—we can save up to 15% on fuel costs. Simple measures include checking your tyres are at the right pressure and that you are driving at the right speed.

[#84] **Moving from grey fleet to green fleet**

Many councils will, on occasion, find it highly convenient to allow staff to use their private vehicles for business travel—commonly known as the 'grey fleet'. In terms of administration and sometimes cost, paying a fixed mileage allowance for the use of a private car is the simplest solution rather than providing pool cars or arranging for a daily rental vehicle. However, there are several issues relating to grey fleet which require careful management.[8]

For instance, employers in many countries may be able to reimburse several cents per mile up to a certain threshold without any tax implications for the employee or insurance implications for the employer. Because this may often involve an office system with an escalator policy by which the more miles you drive the greater the reimbursement becomes, this can encourage staff to drive further and for longer than necessary.

Councils should also consider that for journeys above a certain number of miles per day it might be cheaper (although it may not be perceived as simple) to use a daily rental car rather than requesting employees to use their own vehicle. If, for instance, employees' cars are used for business travel, the employer may have a duty of care to ensure that the car is fit for purpose, is insured for business use and that the employee has a valid driving licence.

Finally, grey fleet vehicles, on average, will be older and create higher emissions than company vehicles or daily rental vehicles which tend to be replaced much more regularly. This, combined with mileage rates, which may create the incentive for additional travel, means that councils should look carefully at the impact grey fleet travel has on total emissions.

So, in summary, by switching from a grey fleet to a green fleet your council might be able to save money and reduce emissions. Now, having looked at grey fleet, we examine the role of smarter driving for your council, by looking at a case study from Merseyside in the UK.

8 Energy Saving Trust, www.est.org.uk, accessed April 2010.

[#7] Smarter driving: Knowsley Metropolitan Borough Council, UK

Knowsley is part of the Liverpool City Region in Merseyside, with a population of 150,000. High-quality infrastructure lends itself to key automotive, manufacturing and service industries which are housed in the borough's many business parks. Major employers include the world-renowned Jaguar Land Rover vehicle plant. At the same time, Knowsley is ranked as one of the most deprived areas in the UK in terms of economic welfare and social cohesion but, despite these challenges, the borough has been recognised nationally for a number of key achievements, ranging from schooling and children's play, to green spaces and kitchen food waste recycling.

These achievements reflect the fact that the council takes sustainability matters very seriously, as illustrated by the fact that per capita CO_2 emissions in the borough are below national average. In addition, both climate change and environmental policy compliance are categorised as corporate group risks and a dedicated Sustainable Resources Service is responsible for coordinating the delivery of cross-departmental action on a plethora of priorities (ranging from climate adaptation and green spaces to waste collection and fleet and logistics).

One novel element of this has been a green fleet review, in partnership with the Energy Saving Trust (EST), which is contributing to the roll-out of a corporate environmental management system to the ISO 14001 standard. This includes the delivery of so-called 'smarter driving' for staff. While this involves senior management, it is particularly focused on fleet drivers who are the major fuel users (this includes council staff who operate waste collection wagons and road-sweeping or grass-cutting vehicles).

By following a few easy-to-follow driving tips taught in a one-hour session, Knowsley council understands that its staff can lower their fuel consumption by up to 15% and reduce harmful emissions. EST estimates that each driver will save up to US$351 and reduce his or her CO_2 emissions by 613 kg per year. And, given that Knowsley employs 7,500 staff, which includes schools, the potential savings run into hundreds of thousands of pounds.

'We ran this initiative in 2009 and it was a great success, resulting in a saving of over US$300 per driver in fuel costs. This is good for tackling climate change and reduces the burden on the public purse', says John Flaherty, Service Director in Knowsley Council's Neighbourhood Services Directorate, who volunteered to participate in the smarter-driving lessons.

Top tips for smarter driving include:

- Avoid excessive speed: at 85 miles per hour (mph) a car uses approximately 25% more fuel than at 70 mph

- Pump up to cut down: under-inflated tyres create more resistance when your car is moving (which means your engine has to work harder) so more fuel is consumed. Check and adjust your tyre pressures regularly and before long journeys. This will also help to increase the life of your tyres as well as emitting less CO_2

- De-clutter: clutter in your boot is extra weight your engine has to lug around. By removing unnecessary weight, you could reduce your engine's workload

- Stop and start less: every time you stop then start again in a traffic queue the engine uses more fuel and therefore produces more CO_2. Keep an eye on the traffic ahead and slow down early by gently lifting your foot off the accelerator while keeping the car in gear. In this way, the traffic may have started moving again by the time you approach the vehicle in front, so you can then change gear and be on your way

- Reduce revving: modern car engines are designed to be efficient from the moment they are switched on, so revving up like a Formula 1 car in pole position only wastes fuel and increases engine wear. Use your gears wisely by changing up a gear a little earlier to reduce revs. If you drive a diesel car try changing up a gear when the rev counter reaches 2,000 rpm and for a petrol car try changing up at 2,500 rpm

- Idling wastes fuel: when the engine is idling you are wasting fuel and adding to CO_2 emissions. If you are likely to be at a standstill for more than 3 minutes, simply switch off the engine

Council officers undertaking the smarter-driving lessons has an additional benefit for the wider community of Knowsley, as 60% of the council's 7,500 employees live in the authority, and may apply the learning domestically as well as at work.

Learning and action from the smarter-driving lessons also sits alongside recommendations from a wider green fleet review including use of the council's grey fleet as well as the procurement of replacement fleet in accordance with new EU regulations on emissions standards. Additionally, this will also coincide with trials of the use of alternative vehicle fuel, a locally sourced, 'first of its kind in the UK' synthetic diesel produced from reclaimed waste in the borough. Flaherty concludes:

> The benefit of being involved in this pilot for the Council is that it reduces our carbon emissions, and diverts waste from landfill. Our broader approach to green fleet management will also support low-carbon technology clusters operating within the authority's business parks so it is great news for local employment and skills development too.

For further information visit www.knowsley.gov.uk (accessed 16 September 2010).

Building on the smarter-driving insights, one can also return to 'carrot' rather than 'stick' incentives for reducing fuel.

[#85] Frequent fleet miles points, with a difference

Similar to the well-known 'air miles' reward system for frequent flyers, why not adopt a similar scheme, but with a major difference?

Create an internal competition among fleet drivers (possibly via a league table that is posted in a visible place such as the staff canteen). To do well drivers need to have used the least fuel and the winners receive a financial award which is paid for by part of the money the council saves from the reduced fuel consumption.

Give it a trial and see how well it works for you!

In the final section of this chapter we offer insights on how your council can enable residents, companies and visitors to travel more sustainably.

11.4 **Public travel**

The business case for different audiences to be motivated to use, or support, public transport initiatives will vary. Businesses will be motivated by an opportunity to cut traffic congestion, although the driver or local residents may be additionally spurred on by the health benefits of more exercise or by improving local air quality through removing exhaust emissions. In contrast, businesses may also be attracted to the return on investment from adopting a green fleet approach similar to that proposed for the council above.

And, while in terms of public travel, grand urban designs may be beyond the scope of this book, given our selection of cost-neutral interventions with modest payback periods, there still remain a number of interesting actions you can take.

We detail these here in respect of walking promotions, cycling rights of way and car-free zones, as well as eco-labelling, alternative fuel sources and integrated planning. We begin with pedestrianisation and walking schemes in Romania.

[#32] **Walking weekends in Craiova, Romania**

The municipality pedestrianises downtown Craiova at weekends to transform it into a recreation area. People of all ages then use the space for anything from walking, roller-skating or as a playground for children (Civitas 2010). As part of city hall's wider 'We Get People Moving' campaign, there will also be a transformation of the city centre with many points of vehicle access with new street-ball courts for basketball and football.

Next we move from walking to cycling as the preferred mode of travel, starting with an example from Amsterdam. It comes as no surprise that the Netherlands is a world leader in cycling, as shown by a comparison of the number of journeys made by bicycle with other countries in Europe, for instance, as detailed in Figure 11.4 (European Conference of Ministers for Transport 2004).

FIGURE 11.4 **Journeys made by bicycle in Europe (%)**

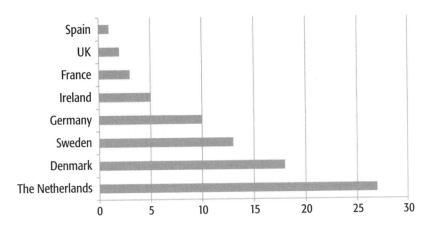

[#33] Cycling rights of way in Amsterdam, the Netherlands

In 2007, Amsterdam became the first Western industrialised city where the number of journeys taken by bicycle exceeded those by cars (Brown 2009). Cyclists have rights too! The primary reason for this is that extensive rights of way exist, along with ample bicycle parking, full integration with public transport and comprehensive education and training of cyclists and motorists.

All of which serves to make driving less attractive than cycling in the city centre. Similar approaches have also proved successful in Denmark and Germany.

What is very apparent from the Amsterdam example is that pedestrian and cycling rights of way are fundamental to successful public transport strategies, and so your council needs to be clear on its policy position and ensuring actions.

This brings us to other innovative cycling practices, namely cargo bikes and bike clubs.

[#86, #34] **A bicycle made for four! And bike clubs in Barcelona, Spain**

Have you and your kids tried the 'cargo bike' yet? You should. Inspired by more cycling trailblazers from the Netherlands, the originally named *bakfiets* is a specifically designed bike that allows adults to go shopping with their children and carry a shop load at the same time. So there are no more excuses not to the leave the car at home!

Although Spain props up the bottom of European cycling rates (Fig. 11.4), Barcelona continues to excel as a world leader on sustainability issues, and is not overlooking the importance of cycling through its bike-sharing scheme known as Bici.[9] For members, the first half-hour of use is free, and services can be bundled together with other public transport amenities such as season tickets. Just as impressively, one-third of all trips in the city are taken on foot (Grist 2007).

Finally, we move from cycling to focus on car eradication, temporarily at least.

[#35, #36, #37] **Car-free areas in New York, Freiburg and Paris**

In the USA, as part of New York's 'PlanNYC 2030', a long-term sustainability vision by the council, car-free Sundays have been introduced downtown. The vision is supported by the Campaign for New York's Future, a coalition of community, civic, business, labour, environmental and health organisations.[10]

---

9 Global Alliance for EcoMobility, ICLEI, www.ecomobility.org, accessed April 2010.

10 www.ecomobility.org

Freiburg in Germany has adopted a whole area-based approach where entire neighbourhoods such as the Vauban district are designated as a car-free zone (Grist 2007).

In comparison, Paris, France, has adopted the novel approach of restricting vehicle access by introducing temporary speed limits on very hot days, to cut air pollution (East 2004).

Of course, all the above should complement wider public awareness campaigning on the adverse sustainability impact of the car if it remains the preferred choice of transport. This relates both to the benefits of buying a fuel-efficient car and smarter driving, as discussed earlier. The former brings us to our latest tip in this chapter.

[#87] Car fuel-economy labelling

Studies show that substantial CO_2 and fuel savings could be achieved if we all purchased the most fuel-efficient car in class. In the case of vans, this could be as much as 17% (Department for Transport 2009). Consequently, a number of countries such as Japan and New Zealand have launched car fuel-economy labels to help customers in their decision-making.

This presents an opportunity for your council to intervene by either raising awareness of these labels among your residents, or in the absence of a national label, collating examples of good practice and benchmarks from industry. In the case of the latter, you should refer back to the national emissions standards touched on earlier in this chapter.

In terms of community messaging one can lean on existing communication campaigns, networks and pathways here, such as community newsletters and so on, ensuring that messages complement any national campaigns (in the same way it was important when providing communications advice on energy or waste reduction in Chapters 8 and 10, respectively).

Finally, while your council may be limited in its financial or political ability to commit to new major infrastructure projects, you still have a pivotal role to play in enabling positive change through integrated planning and other partnership-based working within your authority boundaries.

[#88] Partnerships for integration

As we have seen from Knowsley and other councils, your role in integrated transport planning—road, rail, cycling and walking as well as spatial planning, industrial logistics and possible low-carbon trade zones—is vital to success. It may not necessarily involve spending more money, but rather bringing partners together to share data, learning or agree priorities for collaboration.

Related to this is an innovation from the private sector in relation to co-distribution by two or more companies who come together to share a freight distribution network where their goods are being transported from and to the same locations. There are a number of benefits of such a partnership approach including the opportunity to lower overheads by spreading the cost of investment and also to reduce emissions at the same time.

So, does your council have a role to play in facilitating similar share distribution schemes in your area? Perhaps this is an agenda item for the first or next meeting of the environmental business club we discussed in Chapter 8 on economic development? Other ideas may relate to home-based work or teleworking, whereby IT-enabled communications reduce the need to travel to meetings or at all.

Key learning

✓ Getting a grip on employee, council and public travel can save you money, boost health and quality of life and will reduce costly emissions and congestion.

✓ Potential big wins can be realised in business travel in particular from switching from a grey fleet to a green fleet and from smarter driving.

✓ An integrated approach to transport planning means deciding the car is no longer 'king'.

✓ Novel forms of working should be explored, including alternative fuel choices and facilitating business to pool transportation resources.

✓ We now move to the final chapter in this section, community management.

12

Community management

I wanted to experience both the importance and the difficulties of child raising. I want to set an example that other men will follow (Hironobu Narisawa, Mayor of Tokyo's Bunkyo Ward, 2010, after becoming Japan's first local government chief to take paternity leave).

Typical sustainability actions and outcomes	Cost-neutral interventions
12.1 Localism, neighbourhood vitality and self-help	#38, #39, #40
12.2 Role models that we can all believe in	#8, #89, #90
12.3 Education and well-being	#91 ,#41, #42, #92, #93
12.4 A more sustainable domestic life	#94, #95, #96, #97, #43, #98, #99, #100, #101, #44, #102

12.1 Localism, neighbourhood vitality and self-help

Our opening chapter in this section focused on leadership—by officers and elected members alike—and so it is appropriate to return to this in the final chapter of this section. However, to do this we must focus on how you can nurture and support your neighbourhoods' capacity building and self-help.

As always, we draw attention to cost-neutral and high-impact interventions and will examine four core themes: namely, localism and community participation, trustworthy role models, education and well-being, and low-carbon domestic life. This will include examining a number of key issues such as deprivation, crime, equality and diversity, health, food, energy and water (as waste and transport have already been dealt with in Chapters 10 and 11, we will only cross-reference them here).

To begin, the role of communities to actively govern and manage neighbourhoods and their associated resources—'localism'—is absolutely fundamental to achieving sustainability. According to Boyle (2009), this is because local people and frontline staff have invaluable experience and skills, are more able to solve problems and so local public services should be organised in ways to harness this. With this in mind, let us look at issues of governance first before then turning to management.

As we touched on in Chapter 2, the management by local villages of community forests in the Philippines through landscape alliances (or what Ostrom [1990] refers to as common pool resources [CPRs]) was a vital ingredient in resolving a pressing challenge. But what exactly are CPRs in practice? How replicable are they? And in what way can they benefit leaders in local government? These questions are teased out in the following example from Japan.

[#38] **Common pool resources in Hirano, Nagaike and Yamanoka, Japan**

For centuries, Japan has had extensive common lands of meadows and forests which have been regulated by local village institutions—what Ostrom defines as common pool resources (CPRs). About 3 million hectares are still managed in this way today and one would struggle to find an example of a CPR that has suffered ecological destruction says Ostrom (1990).

Villagers are required by these local village institutions to perform collective work to enhance and maintain the yield of the CPR (such as annual burning or cutting of timber for thatch) and each household has an obligation to contribute a share to such efforts. In the instance of a household failing to perform its share of work, fines are imposed by the local village institution, but they involve making a 'donation' to the village schools.

The long-term success of these locally designed rule systems indicates that it is not necessary for regulation of the CPRs to be imposed coercively from outside by national government, as local 'self-policing' works well.

Ostrom suggests a number of design principles illustrated by long-enduring CPR institutions:

- Clearly defined boundaries. Individuals or households who have rights to withdraw resources from the CPR must be defined, as must the boundaries of the CPR itself

- Alignment between rules of appropriation and provision and local conditions. Appropriation rules restricting time, place, technology or quantity of resource are related to local conditions and to provision rules requiring labour, material or money

- Collective-choice arrangements. Most individuals affected by the operational rules can participate in modifying the rules

- Monitoring. Designated monitors, who actively audit CPR conditions and appropriate behaviour, are accountable to the appropriators or are the appropriators

- Graduated sanctions. Appropriators who violate operational rules are likely to be assigned graduated sanctions, depending on the seriousness and context of the offence, by other appropriators, by officials accountable to the appropriators, or both

- Conflict-resolution mechanisms. Appropriators and their officials have rapid access to low-cost arenas to resolve conflicts among appropriators or between appropriators and officials

- Minimal recognition of rights to organise. The rights of appropriators to devise their own institutions are not challenged by national government authorities

The take-out for you is that this tried-and-tested approach to collaborative governance has worked in a number of municipalities in different countries ranging from the Philippines, Spain and Switzerland to Japan, and so would appear to lend itself to being replicated elsewhere. Perhaps this is something you might pilot on one of your council's natural resources, for instance, a fishing lake?

Accepting that CPRs are valuable, how do we move from the governance of a single resource to embrace a broader neighbourhood involvement role? There are fine examples of innovations to stimulate public consultation, such as the following example from Colombia (Forum for the Future 2010).

[#39] **Local solutions competition in Bogotá, Colombia**

The city administration of Bogotá realised that they needed new ideas to address their challenges. So they developed 'actions for coexistence'—a competition that invited community groups and residents to propose local solutions to locally identified problems.

The competition is more than simply an idea-generating exercise. Local officials are committed to report progress back to community groups as to how their opinions on coexistence shaped the council's planning.

However community participation is not the same as community management, as Power and Houghton (2007) discuss in detail through the positive experiences of Copenhagen and other forward-thinking municipalities.

[#40] **People-centric neighbourhood management in Copenhagen, Denmark**

'Currently, a child born into a family living in a deprived area will leave school earlier, earn less and die younger than the rest of the population. People's fates should not be inscribed so indelibly on their birth certificates', say Power and Houghton (2007).

Neighbourhood management can help resolve this. Neighbourhood management invites joined-up working with education, youth, health and social services to tackle problems directly and support preventive action together. The most effective neighbourhood management organisations broker local service agreements on 'street services' that affect neighbourhood conditions, such as the police, the environment, cleansing and refuse, leisure, parks and repairs.

Crucially, Power and Houghton found that, under most scenarios, neighbourhood management pays for itself through a reduction in vandalism, lower insurance premiums, better repairs, increased property values and enhanced physical attractiveness. Essential components of neighbourhood management include:

- Neighbourhood manager. Has high status and acts as community liaison

- Local office. An organisational base and information point

- Cooperation with other public services. Across the police, health and education services

- Community representatives. Arrange local agreements and local boards

Copenhagen is cited as an outstanding example here, in terms of how long-term planning, careful urban design and understanding of public space lends itself to high-quality neighbourhoods. Through strong neighbourhood management, areas that had previously been dissected by roads or used for car-parking were converted into new people-friendly spaces.

The above ways of working are intended to operate in tandem with council officers and elected members, who would provide network support and political leadership, respectively.

Clearly, although hugely beneficial, this is not easy and requires an appetite for a shift in the balance of power.

The significant benefit is that it would facilitate the development of integrated, authority-wide local area agreements that harness the vitality of neighbourhoods across the council, yield total solutions that improve performance and avoid inefficiencies and promote self-help.

12.2 Role models that we can all believe in

As we saw in the previous section, members of the community with high status are a crucial component of making neighbourhoods work and although there is no 'set formula' for what makes such a person tick, we can tease out some valuable common characteristics. The following characteristics should be sought and encouraged among local authority residents:

- Organising skills

- Speaking up for the voiceless

- Challenging the status quo

Each of these is now explored further in turn. We begin with organising skills, drawing on a remarkable case study from a community leader in Canada's Fort Chipewyan.

[#8] Global campaign to safeguard local health and culture: Fort Chipewyan, Canada

Fort Chipewyan, commonly referred to as The Fort, is a hamlet in northern Alberta, Canada, under the jurisdiction of the regional municipality of Wood Buffalo.

Recognised as Alberta's oldest community, Fort Chipewyan is located on the extreme north-western tip of Lake Athabasca. Heavily dependent on air transport, the community is served by a regional airport. Fort Chipewyan ranks as the second largest community in the municipality, with a population of 1,012. The hamlet's population is predominantly made up of Cree First Nations, Chipewyan (Dene) First Nations and Métis people. Resource industries are the major source of employment for residents, along with government (health, education and social service jobs) and a growing tourism industry linked to nearby Wood Buffalo National Park.

In recent years, oil companies have increasingly invested in the extraction of oil from what local community leaders refer to as 'toxic' unconventional fuels, such as tar sands and shale oil. It is alleged that the extraction of these fuels produces significantly higher CO_2 emissions compared with 'conventional' fuels—some processes emitting up to eight times more CO_2.

'We no longer call it "dirty oil" we call it "bloody oil"—it is killing people, and seriously harming the entire future of my people's culture by destroying the land at the same time', says former Mikisew Chief George Poitras, who is fighting for his people as an anti-oil sands activist.

Tar sands consist of oil trapped in a complex mixture of sand, water and clay. The extraction and production of oil from tar sands emits on average three times as much carbon dioxide as the extraction and production of conventional oil. Canada has proven tar sand reserves of 174 billion barrels of oil, second only to Saudi Arabia's conventional reserves. Shale oil consists of oil trapped in sedimentary rock, which is released when the rock is superheated. Shale oil extraction emits up to eight times more carbon dioxide than conventional oil extraction. Shale oil exploitation is still at the research and development stage, but millions of dollars are being invested to make it viable.

Poitras has encouraged people—inside and outside of Fort Chipewyan—to shake off their fears and speak out for their children and grandchildren. In 2010 the campaign resulted in a social film being screened across cinemas across the world to make a global audience aware of this campaign. It includes narration by the Hollywood star Neve Campbell, a fellow Canadian, who felt compelled to support and act. The campaign brings together a collective of community groups, NGOs and responsible business leaders including WWF, Fair Pensions and The Co-operative Group. Campaigners are calling on anyone who has a pension to ask their provider not to invest in tar sands.

'As our Cree elders say—what are we going to say to our grandchildren, that we didn't do anything because we didn't have the courage?' continues Poitras, who goes on to conclude:

We strongly believe that tar sands development is linked to unexplained high incidences of cancers in humans and the fish and game birds which have traditionally made up our staple diet for thousands of years. So, we as community leaders are accountable to the collective community mobilising serious action when it is a matter of life and death.

For more information visit:
- www.woodbuffalo.ab.ca (accessed 16 September 2010)
- www.co-operativecampaigns.co.uk/toxicfuels (accessed 30 September 2010)

So, it is evident from Poitras's passionate campaigning on behalf of his community that he had the status and determination to step up and act as the liaison between residents and the outside world. In addition to being inspired by this case study in terms of nurturing your local neighbourhood champions, there is another practical action you can take to help Poitras—ask your pension fund manager if your money is being invested in companies who are engaged in tar sands!

In terms of speaking up for the voiceless, councils can play another pivotal role in ensuring that irresponsible private sector actions are not allowed to harm the communities we serve. As a case in point we look at the shocking issue of unethical firms targeting children to make a huge profit, through the sexualisation of children's merchandise (Mayo and Nairn 2009). Harming our children (for instance, by reinforcing negative stereotypes about young girls) damages the fabric of our communities and inhibits our ability to develop the leaders of tomorrow. So we propose actions you can take to protect such vulnerable groups through school education programmes and your procurement frameworks.

[#89] **Non-consumer kids**

Are you a parent? If so, do you know which companies your children are talking to and about what? Mayo and Nairn's research on 'consumer kids' highlights that the commercial world can manipulate the preferences and spending patterns of children in a startling and damaging way.

Children can be a captive audience for sophisticated and energetic marketing techniques because they spend so much of their day online or in front of the television; they suffer from peer pressure, have an underdeveloped sense of self and a lack of experience of the real world. For example, on average British children spend five hours and 18 minutes watching television, playing computer games or online each day. The annual total of 2,000 hours overshadows the 900 hours spent in class and also the 1,270 hours in the company of their parents. The harmful effects of this are that in our child population the more materialistic children are, the more likely they are to suffer from low self-esteem and poor family relationships.

According to the research, while parents appear to be waking up to the threat of sexual predators online, they have no concept of how business grooms their children for profit. Corporate techniques include the sexualisation of merchandise or marketing campaigns, particularly targeting young girls, to persuade children to buy through the sheer power of peer pressure.

Children are 'recruited' through enhanced membership schemes or special offers to promote products to their friends, while websites that are popular with children are peppered with advertisements made to look like content. Personal information is routinely sought, often as a condition of getting access to a site.

The book also reveals startling new data on the dominance of the media on children's lives, saying that it is hard for young people to escape from big business. That makes it far easier for business to obtain information and give children, including young children, a heavy sales pitch under the cover of entertainment. For instance, one piece of research found that 85% of popular children's websites collected some sort of personal information, including email address, user name, postcode, date of birth, gender and age. Most of this information is 'compulsory', meaning that the child cannot use parts of the site without handing over these details. Shockingly, about 15% of sites require information to take part at all and another 35% offer ringtones, wallpaper, newsletters and screensavers in exchange for information.

Mayo and Nairn say that the size of the market for children's consumer goods means that companies will stop at nothing to get information. They estimate that the total market stands at about US$148.5 billion, up 33% in the past five years, with US$18 billion of this coming from pocket money. So parents, teachers and other authorities need to be alert to this and take the appropriate action to protect children.

This important call to action for parents and teachers to address the problem of 'consumer kids' has implications for you as public servants, too. Your council can play a key role in stemming the tide; by getting the message out to educators and also as part of sustainable procurement you can review your approved suppliers to check what their child protection policies are.

In closing this section, we consider those who challenge the status quo. This is done by delving into the opening quote attributable to Hironobu Narisawa, Mayor of Tokyo's Bunkyo Ward. It again touches on gender stereotypes and raises an interesting challenge to societal perceptions about 'traditional' roles (Bouthier 2010).

[#90] **Taking paternity leave**

A few days' paternity leave may not seem like a matter of national importance, but for Hironobu Narisawa, the mayor of a Tokyo district, it is a major development for Japanese society.

In June 2010 he became Japan's first local government chief to take time off work to look after a child, a move the mayor hopes will inspire other men to do the same.

According to Bouthier (2010), Japanese law allows either parent to take leave of up to one year after childbirth, but almost all of those who do so are women, perhaps a reflection of traditional gender roles that remain entrenched. For instance, no male employees of Bunkyo ward are currently on paternity leave and nationally only 1.2% of fathers take advantage of paternity leave.

What does this mean for your council? Take paternity leave yourself (as appropriate) or support and encourage others to take paternity leave! Share the news about paternity leave with young males and females alike, perhaps through staff inductions and awareness initiatives to help change perceptions and culture.

Wrapping this all together we can see being a role model can be very tough as it impacts on your personal and professional life. However, your role in nurturing tomorrow's community leaders is an extremely important one and comes at no cost other than your time and personal will.

12.3 Education and well-being

Education and well-being covers a broad range of issues.

We have already touched on the work of schools throughout the book—including consumer kids (above) and eco-schools (as part of Chapter 10 on waste)—as well as the role of green spaces in promoting health (in Chapter 9 on economic development and planning). So, building on this, our focus here is:

- Inter-generational and inter-cultural play

- The role of food nutrition in cutting carbon and poverty

- Family planning and sustainable consumption

As we saw when looking at the value of green spaces, as well as being able to cater for leisure and health needs, green spaces can also offer help on social cohesion. This constitutes our first tip here.

[#91] Social cohesion through play for everyone

Green spaces provide a public space where people of all ages and from all walks of life can share leisure time. Interestingly, this can happen by accident or design. Why not make it by design? Your motivation may be to break down inter-generational or inter-cultural barriers to social cohesion.

Organised 'play' can help here. As part of a wider events calendar, organise specific activities aimed at bringing young and old or different ethnic groups together. This could be something as simple as kite-making, bowling, a walking club or a family picnic. Best of all, it is fun and it can be tailored to the local area, such as events celebrating an important festival, commemorating a local hero or celebrating sporting success for a local team.

Planning for food nutrition can play a powerful role in reducing our carbon footprint, alleviating poverty and assisting with social cohesion. We now consider two separate of examples of this in practice.

[#41] 'Field to table' in Toronto, Canada

Toronto-based FoodShare is a coalition of civic, municipal and education activists striving to build consensus for policies that provide every Canadian with enough money and knowledge to buy the basic and right food they need, and establish it as a human right.[11]

FoodShare leads on a number of community-based strategies such as wholesale bulk-buying clubs, cooperatives, backyard gardening and good food box programmes to extend people's food buying power. Educational campaigns, stressing the importance of eating in relation to overall health as well as environmental sustainability, have also been launched in schools, community centres and workplaces.

This 'Field to Table Schools' initiative has proved to be particularly popular; governing boards are called to reinvigorate home economics classes for their students, with all high-school graduates needing to demonstrate cooking, shopping and food budgeting skills through interactive lessons. Here both boys and girls receive cooking training, in the home and at school. Schools are also requested to work to transform their own environments and student eating practices by establishing schoolyard gardens, in which students can grow food in order to supplement their diet during the school day.

11 FoodShare, 'Field to Table Schools', www.foodshare.net/school02.htm, accessed April 2010.

This schools-oriented work is complemented by attempts to change the environment in which children live back at home too. Here community-based programmes such as cooking classes, community kitchens and ovens, cooking groups and baby-food-making classes are established in order to facilitate nutritious eating and communal cooking, especially for the elderly, low-income, street youth and specific ethnic groups. Communities and neighbourhoods are also asked to regularly host communal cooking events such as barbecues, bread-baking and soup-making to encourage greater community cohesion.

So learning from the Toronto example, what can your council do that is helpful? Well, again, through existing networks you can team up with local groups to develop similar educational initiatives. This would sit alongside or even be part of any sustainable schools initiatives. Again, all that this requires is some of your time.

Staying with the topic of food: for some, eating less meat is a good way to improve food nutrition, as the example from the State of Michigan (2010) demonstrates.

[#42] **Meatout day in Michigan, USA**

The following statement from the Governor of Michigan explains their new 'meatout day' campaign.

> Whereas, A wholesome diet of vegetables, fruits, and whole grains promotes good health and reduces the risk of heart disease, stroke, cancer, diabetes, and other chronic diseases, which take the lives of approximately 1.3 million Americans each year; and,

> Whereas, The number of those who choose to live the lifestyle of a vegan or vegetarian has increased and so has the availability and selection of meat and dairy alternatives in mainstream grocery stores, restaurants, and catering operations; and,

> Whereas, Reducing the consumption of meat or not eating meat at all can significantly decrease the exposure to infectious pathogens such as salmonella, *E. coli*, and

campylobacter, which take the lives of several thousand Americans and sicken millions more each year; and,

Whereas, The benefits of a plant-based diet can consist of increased energy levels, lower food budget costs, and simplified food preparation and cleanup; and,

Whereas, It is encouraged that the residents of this state get into the habit of healthy living by consuming a diet that is rich with vegetables, fruit, and whole grains, and by staying active;

Now, Therefore, be it Resolved, That I, Jennifer M. Granholm, governor of the state of Michigan, do hereby proclaim March 20 2010, Michigan Meatout Day in Michigan. In observance of this day, I encourage the residents of this state to choose not to eat meat. Eating a healthy diet can be fun. Explore the different recipes that can be created by using fresh ingredients and by having a sense of adventure.

As you can see, the bold declaration from Senator Granholm is intended to raise awareness among residents of the health benefits of not eating meat. Quite controversial too, especially to local meat farmers!

But health is only part of a rationale for opting out of meat, as well as dairy products. For instance, see Figure 12.3, which looks at the GHG emissions arising from various foodstuffs. As you can see, meat and dairy are much greater emitters than potato or wheat, for example.

So, taking the Michigan example and Vaze's statistics together you could propose a campaign. Start with a 'no meat or dairy products day' once per year, with the aim of moving it to once per month and then once per week. You may also decide not to include fish in this opt-out, given that for types of fish such as herring, the emissions arising are lower than for bread wheat, as we can see in Figure 12.3. If you operate in a region where the local diet tends to be meat-free anyway—such as in certain parts of India or a region where insects (which produce up to ten times less emissions than livestock) are a staple part of the diet such as in Ghana (e.g. fried winged termites; Carrington 2010)—you may choose to focus your attention on non-protein or low-emitting food products. For instance, in terms of the former, the emissions arising from potatoes are lower than from oil seed rape, as we can also see from Figure 12.3. Try it, and see how well it works!

FIGURE 12.3 **GHG emissions from different foods**

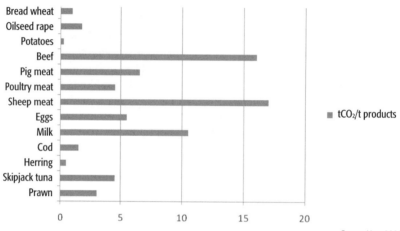

Source: Vaze 2009

While the Vaze data is informative, it raises a broader discussion about localism, also teased out by Santa Monica's 'buy local' campaign referred to in Chapter 8. That is, there needs to be some balance in the system, given there are potentially wider sustainability issues at play here, and so you may be called on to make difficult choices on trade-offs. Take for instance calls in some quarters not to buy fairtrade because of the associated air-freight miles or because it does not support local businesses. The argument against this call is our next example below.

[#92] **Local or seasonal fruit and vegetables 'versus' fairtrade**

The food miles debate poses a real dilemma. Some people believe that climate change is paramount, and so want to 'do their bit' to stop it, buy local and boycott produce from abroad, especially things that are flown in. However, others believe that they should support poor farmers to improve their income and to take care of their families by working and trading their way out of poverty (Forstater *et al.* 2007).

If consumers were to boycott fresh produce air-freighted from Africa, such as fairtrade flowers from Kenya, the UK's total carbon emissions would be reduced by less than 0.1%, but the impact on workers and their communities reliant on this trade would be massively significant.

However, it is not a question of doing one or the other, you can do both, and you should do both. For example, if you want to reduce your emissions from shopping while also continue to support fairtrade, you could choose to reduce your meat consumption or walk instead of driving to the store to shop.

And so, continuing with the theme of controversial theories on approaches to sustainability, let us close this section by returning to the issue of population growth and sustainable consumption (raised at the start of the book by Porritt and Monbiot, in the context of family planning).

[#93] Time to choose: Two kids? Or a dog and a car?

As we know, current levels of consumption are unsustainable and a growing population exacerbates this problem. Add to this heady mix fresh concern over the footprint of family pets which some estimate to emit the carbon emissions of a large car (Vaughan 2010), then perhaps the time has come to ask people to make a choice.

So, do we want to move toward a lifestyle that lends itself to sustainable, 'one planet living' or not? If yes, we all need to understand the footprint of raising children, owning pets or buying cars and come to the conclusion we cannot have it all. Rather, we need to choose.

To be clear, building on Ostrom's (1990) approach to communal governance of natural resources, we are not necessarily proposing a mandated China-esque one-child-per-family policy, but rather suggesting local councils have a role to play in making people aware of the positive choices they can make and asking them to work together to solve the conundrum.

It should also be noted there are no religious ambiguities here as we would be asking residents to abstain from reproduction to support the development of their existing children and fellow neighbours.

All of which sets us up nicely for the final section of this chapter, on sustainability in wider domestic living.

12.4 **A more sustainable domestic life**

Both above, and in previous chapters we have looked at more sustainable forms of living in the home including food, waste and travel. Here we focus our attention now on other major issues, notably domestic energy and water (previously we have only talked about council energy and water in Chapter 8).

As always, the appropriateness of an intervention will depend on your particular circumstance as a council. As with estates management, you will again have to consider your residents' local climate and any national environmental standards. But in terms of housing stock, is it social housing or private? Who builds and owns the homes? Is it the council or a third party? These answers will seriously affect your business case to act, although regardless of your situation, there is still scope for you to do so.

Before moving on to specific examples and guidance, let us first consider the carbon footprint of a 'typical' resident as shown in Figure 12.4 (drawing on the UK as an illustrative example). Footprinting in this way is helpful to understanding how we can move from a potentially unsustainable lifestyle to more sustainable, one-planet way of living. By carbon footprint here we mean the total CO_2 emissions arising from different lifestyle choices ranging from use of a private car to purchase of leisure goods and services. To put this in context, the typical UK person emits approximately 11 tonnes of CO_2—mostly on food, energy and consumer products—while many environmentalists argue that a safe and more equitable footprint would be 5 tonnes per person (Forstater *et al.* 2007). So, there is a very long way to go to get this right!

FIGURE 12.4 **Carbon footprint of a 'typical' resident**

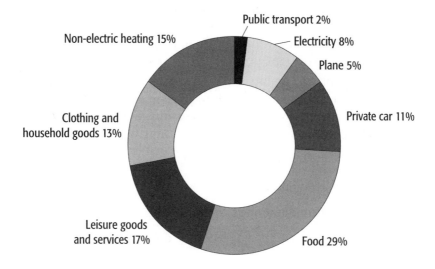

Public transport 2%

Non-electric heating 15%

Electricity 8%

Plane 5%

Clothing and household goods 13%

Private car 11%

Leisure goods and services 17%

Food 29%

Source: Vaze 2009

Although this is an important figure to consider, remember too that this is per person and there are many multi-person households. Also, it is intended to be indicative and the impact will, of course, vary from person to person according to behaviour, wealth and local context as we know.

Given this, we will now consider the following as ways you can assist residents in your council area to reduce their footprint:

- Energy and water use in the home

- Wider lifestyle choices such as holiday air travel

- Other collective community schemes

Starting with energy in the home, you will recall as part of the estates management section in Chapter 8 we reviewed the energy hierarchy, the insulation values of various construction materials, as well as appropriate built environment responses to different local climates.

As such, we will use this platform of knowledge to relate it to the domestic scene.

Fundamentally, for you to propose appropriate energy-efficiency measures for residents in your authority, it is essential to understand what the major sources of energy use, and more importantly, energy loss are, what possible measures are available to the resident and then what interventions would be suitable within the resident's budget for improvements. The improvements should minimise the home's heat loss in the most cost-effective way to reduce heating demand and energy bills, improve comfort and increase the value of the property.

We take each of these in turn below, starting with heat loss.

In a typical uninsulated house the percentage of energy loss is as follows (EST 2008):

- 17% of heat is lost through the roof

- 33% is lost through the walls

- 20% is lost through the windows

- 10% is lost through the floor and the door

- 20% is lost due to draughts and essential ventilation

Space heating (to warm different parts of the home) and hot water production account for approximately three-quarters of overall domestic energy use and carbon emissions, with the remainder made up by lighting, appliances and cooking (DCLG 2006).

Energy-efficiency improvement measures for existing homes fall into four main categories: improving insulation, improving air leakage, improving heating systems and improving electrical systems (De Montfort University 2010). Using industry best practice Table 12.4 proposes simple, cost-neutral, energy-efficiency improvements for the home.

[#94] **Simple energy-efficiency improvements in the home**

The starting premise here is that any energy-efficiency improvement in the home should be of a reasonable cost of less than US$1,500 in total, with a payback period of no greater than five years and will not cause excessive disruption to lifestyle. (But again, this is intended to be illustrative, noting different residents will have different budgets.)

TABLE 12.4 **Domestic energy-efficiency improvements**

Appropriate improvement	Supporting comments	Saving (£/year)	Installation cost (£)	Payback period (years)
A new condensing boiler	Replace your energy-inefficient gas-fired back boiler and hot water cylinder	US$300–325	US$1,500	3–5 (average)
Install heating control package	The timer on your boiler has only two settings, so it fails to vary with seasonal temperature changes for example	US$75–90	US$300	3
Improved hot water tank insulation	Replace your loose-fitting hot water tank jacket	US$30	US$15	0.5
Add more loft insulation (up to 250–300 mm)	Only 50 mm is currently in place	US$60–75	US$360	4–5
Install low-energy lighting	Replace your old tungsten lighting with new energy efficient lamps	US$60–75	US$360	Less than 1
Draught-proofing	You do not make any mention of this and so a precursory check is in order	US$22.5–30	US$112.5	2–3

The internal insulation of walls, installation of double or triple glazing for windows and mechanical ventilation systems (for cool, fresh air) have been ruled out for the time being on the grounds that they would be both costly and cause significant disruption.

In addition to these technological interventions, you should also consider advice to your residents on positive behaviour change actions: for instance, handy hints such as remembering not to leave unused appliances on standby, which unnecessarily wastes energy and money.

Again, renewable technologies should only be considered after carrying out all the basic energy-efficiency improvements. The cost and payback period for renewable technologies is also likely to be significantly greater, so all things being equal, it is recommended that no installations of this type are made for now. However, it may become feasible should you become eligible for grant support (for example, through national government funding or PAYS schemes). In such a case, depending on both your climate and natural environment, solar water heating (SWH) and ground source heat pumps (GSHP) could be an attractive option. SWH systems use heat from the sun to provide hot water in homes, while GSHP use heat from the ground to provide hot water or space heat.

However, even the modest improvements suggested above are far out of reach for any of your residents who are living in poverty. In such circumstances, the following low-tech actions can be taken. Remember, it can all make a big difference!

[#95, #96, #97] Low-tech, energy-saving solutions

The list below are zero-cost, low-tech ideas for those with little or no money and are a mix of the simple and somewhat radical (various sources, including EST 2010 and Yarrow 2008):

- Manual control of thermostat. Try turning down the temperature by 1°C in the colder months of the year; this can save up to 10% of energy consumption

- Liberate your radiators. Move large pieces of furniture away from radiators and fit reflective panels behind them. You can make your own panel using a recycled piece of aluminium foil with cardboard and this can increase efficiency by 20%

- Switch off. Remember not to leave the televisions or other electronic appliances on standby, switch off lights when leaving a room for a considerable period of time

- Homemade draught excluders. Take old newspapers or socks, tightly pack them into an old pair of tights. Place the excluder on the floor just inside front and back doors

- Benefit from solar gain. Open curtains at dawn and close them at dusk

- Clean refrigeration. Keeping the coils at the back of a fridge or freezer dust free will increase efficiency by up to 30%

- The big cook. If preparing hot food, it is more efficient to do a multi-meal bake as opposed to one meal at a time, then store or freeze the rest

- Careful washing. Avoid using the dishwasher and wash all clothes at 30°C (explored in detail below)

- Brighter evenings. Refine the times when you get up in the morning and go to bed at night to fit in with the season's available daylight to make use of natural light! (explored in detail below)

We explore the last two tips in more detail here.

A 'Climate Wash at 30°C' campaign led by the retailer Marks & Spencer since 2008 has proved to be a big success in the UK; about 70% of own-branded clothing is labelled with this recommendation (Ethical Corporation 2009). Such moves are important as about 75% of the carbon footprint of clothing is washing, drying and ironing. Washes carried out at 30°C instead of 40°C have saved 25,000 tonnes of CO_2 during 2008–2009, with 31% of customers agreeing to take action.

The benefit for your residents of washing at 30°C is that it can reduce the energy consumption of the washing machine by up to 40%, thus cutting down on household bills.

Brighter evenings could also help meet your carbon emissions targets by saving almost 500,000 tonnes of CO_2 each year (the equivalent to taking 185,000 cars off the road permanently). To that end, the 10:10 climate change campaign has launched its Lighter Later campaign (10:10 2010). It wants clocks shifted so that Britons gain an extra hour of daylight in the evenings, all year round. That means shifting to Greenwich Mean Time (GMT) plus one hour in winter and GMT+2 hours in summer. The extra hour of daylight in the evening saves energy because people would use artificial light for a smaller portion of the day. Campaigners at 10:10 say that changing daylight hours would also have social as well as environmental benefits. It could prevent 100 fatalities a year on the country's roads, according to scientists (10:10 2010), and up to 80,000 jobs could be created in the tourism and leisure sectors, bringing an extra US$3.7–5.25 billion into the economy each year.

But remember: you do not have to wait for the clocks to change. You can refine your routine according to daylight hours!

Deciding whether your residents can afford a retrofit or must pursue a low-tech solution, or a combination of both, will depend on *who* pays and *how*. So, to help remove barriers for taking action, we propose two ways forward here that are both cost-neutral. First, if the housing is council-owned stock then one can apply the PAYS techniques outlined under estates management. If private housing then you could examine the scope to partner with a commercial contractor as shown from the following example from Berlin in Germany.

[#43] Removing costs for housing retrofits in Berlin, Germany

The Berlin Energy Agency in Germany is part owned by the City of Berlin and organises large retrofits using special contracts with service companies that remove the upfront cost to the building owners (Forum for the Future 2009b). Similarly, Kirklees RE-Charge, UK, offers secured loans from Kirklees Council to households for energy generation, repayable upon the sale of the house.

Having looked at the buildings themselves, we also need to examine consumer products used within the home.

[#98] **Making consumer electronics green**

When suggesting to residents that they replace appliances, specify those that carry the energy-saving recommended label, such as the US Energy Star or EU Energy Label. Priority products are those with high energy consumption, such as the fridge freezer, television, washing machine and computer (Vaze 2009).

Focusing on computers, you should also future-proof your advice given the growing emissions arising from IT, as a result of the growth of online social networks and devices such as the Apple iPad (Greenpeace 2010). Again, recommend those that carry the energy-saving recommended label.

Having looked at domestic energy, we now look at water in the home and we consider low-tech solutions for those with less money, as well as options to purchase water-saving devices.

[#99] **Low-tech water-saving ideas**

There are a number of ways to save water, and they all start with how you can help your residents modify their behaviour.[12] Handy hints are as follows:

- When washing dishes by hand, do not leave the water running while rinsing

- Run your washing and dishwasher only when they are full. You can save up to 1,000 gallons a month

- Choose plants and groundcovers instead of turf for hard-to-water areas such as steep slopes and isolated strips

- Plant in the seasons when conditions are cooler and rainfall is more plentiful

12 Alliance for Water Efficiency, www.wateruseitwisely.com, accessed April 2010.

- For cold drinks keep a pitcher of water in the refrigerator instead of running the tap. This way, every drop goes down you and not the drain

- Water your lawn and garden in the morning or evening when temperatures are cooler to minimise evaporation

- Wash fruit and vegetables in a pan of water instead of running water from the tap

- Use a broom instead of a hosepipe to clean your drive and pavement and save water every time

- Collect the water you use for rinsing fruit and vegetables, then re-use it to water houseplants

- Shorten showers by a minute or two and you will save up to 150 gallons per month

- Collect water from your roof to water your garden

- Next time you add or replace a flower or shrub, choose a low-water-use plant for year-round landscape colour and save up to 550 gallons each year

- Washing dark clothes in cold water saves both on water and on energy while helping your clothes to keep their colours

- Keep a bucket in the shower to catch water as it warms up or runs. Use this water to flush toilets or water plants.

These all conserve water and save money too!

Now we can look at handy hints for your residents on their lifestyle choices.

[#100] **Making water-using equipment green**

Some refrigerators and air conditioners are cooled with wasted flows of water. So, consider:

- Upgrading with air-cooled appliances for significant water savings

- Buying new appliances that offer cycle and load-size adjustments when yours need replacing. They are more water- and energy-efficient

- Upgrade older toilets with water-efficient models

- Use a water-efficient showerhead. They are inexpensive, easy to install, and can save you up to 750 gallons a month

- Use a hose nozzle or turn off the water while you wash your car. You will save up to 100 gallons every time

- Listen for dripping taps and running toilets. Fixing a leak can save 300 gallons a month or more

- When shopping for a new washing machine, compare resource savings among Energy Star models. Some of these can save up to 20 gallons per load—energy too

- Ask a plumber re-route your grey water to trees and gardens rather than letting it run into the sewer line

- If your toilet was installed more than a couple of decades ago, reduce the amount of water used for each flush by inserting a displacement device in the tank

Now let us turn to the more controversial issue of flying. On fairness grounds, we do not propose an all-out ban or even a request for people to opt out of flying. It does not seem credible, particularly as we see environment ministers continually flying overseas to agree another new global climate agreement! So, what might be a helpful suggestion that would also be desirable?

[#101] **Air travel and holiday options**
If people take a couple of holidays a year, how about asking them to consider having one overseas and another spent in their home country? You could ask them to think about this not for environmental reasons necessarily, but rather to support the domestic

economy during these difficult times—a tourism version of 'buy local'!

You could start by piloting an initiative with your tourist authority.

Let us also look at what actions individuals can take by coming together with fellow residents in the spirit of neighbourhood togetherness, as witnessed in the UK's Ashton Hayes.

> ### [#44] Villagers aim to kick carbon habit in Ashton Hayes, UK
>
> One community that is 'walking the talk' when it comes to more sustainable living is Ashton Hayes, Cheshire, which aspires to become the UK's first carbon-neutral village
>
> 'It's something that has brought the whole community together', says Garry Charnock, one of the organisers of the low-carbon community project. 'Little things—switching off lights, turning down your thermostat—that sort of thing—could make a big change overall if you did it at a community level' (Mukherjee 2009).
>
> The project has managed to reduce household carbon emissions in the village by 23%. Initially, there was some scepticism, including from the local publican, but once Charnock and his team of like-minded residents had shown how you could reduce the pub's energy bills by US$375 by not keeping the cooker running in the morning and switching off the beer cooler when it was winter, they got another convert!
>
> Many people said that the project had benefits way beyond carbon reduction, such as the community spirit that has been generated. 'I've lived in the village for 25 years, and I've met people I've never met before as a result of the project', says Lynn May, a local businesswoman (Mukherjee 2009).
>
> The local authority is supporting the group in a number of ways, such as reprioritising existing budgets to develop a footpath to link the school, other communities and the railway station, encouraging people to cycle or walk instead of taking the car.

Listening to the story from Ashton Hayes residents and picking up the lessons from elsewhere in this chapter, we can see that a bit of community goodwill can go a very long way to making our lifestyles more sustainable. And, crucially, many of these are free to do, if not cost-neutral within a short payback period.

Maybe you could think about piloting a low-carbon community group at your council? Start with a proactive or willing local champion with high status (see Section 12.2 for characteristics of ideal candidates).

Remember: any advice you share with residents must be in line with national educational campaigns. It would be a terrible shame if you ended up confusing residents with competing or contradictory messages. Plus, it saves you time and effort, too! Much better is to join up with such national campaigns, adding your message to the back of this.

Also, you can call on existing communication pathways to spread the word, such as newsletters or regular community newspapers. Another idea is a 'green homes roadshow'.

[#102] **Green homes roadshow**

Nothing convinces people better than their seeing, hearing or feeling the change for themselves. So why not look at piloting a roadshow which takes you and your team out on the road visiting people in community centres, other public spaces or indeed their homes to show them what sustainability measures work and why. This may take the form of water-wise gardening tips or how to use a thermostat effectively.

All of this is simple but powerful stuff, which yet again has a massive impact with regards to hearts and minds, behaviour change, influencing leaders as they see voters taking notice of these issues, and staff morale—there is nothing better than sharing this—especially for the passionate people who may been drawn to working for you as they wanted to make a hands-on difference. This does not mean more costs but rather a reprioritisation of staff time. You may also want to engage your newly established low-carbon community group as willing ambassadors to work with your staff at these events or to even open up their homes for a guided sustainability tour!

So, we have now finished this chapter and indeed this part of the book. We will now discuss how you can manage this myriad of interventions in a coherent way: that is, aligned to your council's core strategy and operations.

Key learning

✓ Effective forms of localism and community participation are key to good governance and neighbourhood management.

✓ Role models with high status will bring residents together and champion sustainability causes—working in tandem with local councillors and officers alike.

✓ Positive action on sustainability contributes to the education and well-being of your residents, such as play that promotes social cohesion.

✓ Simple but high-impact actions can be taken on water and energy conservation that will reduce household bills and save the planet at the same time.

Part IV

OUT OF THE DARKNESS: GOLDEN RULES FOR EXCELLENCE IN AUSTERITY

Route mapping

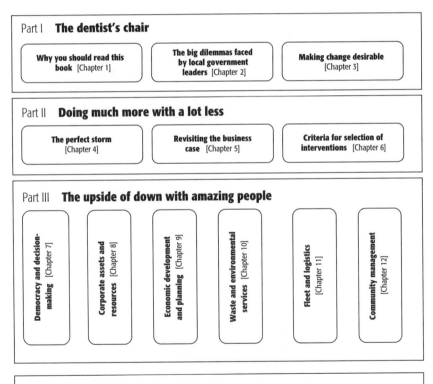

Part I **The dentist's chair**

Why you should read this book [Chapter 1]

The big dilemmas faced by local government leaders [Chapter 2]

Making change desirable [Chapter 3]

Part II **Doing much more with a lot less**

The perfect storm [Chapter 4]

Revisiting the business case [Chapter 5]

Criteria for selection of interventions [Chapter 6]

Part III **The upside of down with amazing people**

Democracy and decision-making [Chapter 7]

Corporate assets and resources [Chapter 8]

Economic development and planning [Chapter 9]

Waste and environmental services [Chapter 10]

Fleet and logistics [Chapter 11]

Community management [Chapter 12]

Part IV **Out of the darkness: golden rules of excellence in austerity**

Battling back [Chapter 13]

Reaffirming what is meant by excellence [Chapter 14]

Over to you [Chapter 15]

13

Battling back

Leaders with passion and drive, who put sustainability at the heart of their vision, can create thriving cities which offer their people a high quality of life, respect their environment, and have the resilience to cope with the changes climate change will bring (Peter Madden, Chief Executive, Forum for the Future, 2008).

Typical sustainability actions and outcomes	Cost-neutral interventions
13.1 Service-based interventions	–
13.2 From learning to mandating	#45

13.1 **Service-based interventions**

As we have seen throughout this book 'battling back' is about doing the best you can given the cards you have been dealt. In Table 13.1 we list the issues and interventions for each service or function covered in Chapters 7 to 12 (note that the long list of over 100 interventions is detailed numerically at the start of the book). You can use this as a checklist for taking action.

TABLE 13.1 Service-led interventions

Your activity	Typical sustainability actions and outcomes	Cost-neutral interventions
Democracy and decision-making	Recalibrating the rules to enable innovation Being able to take the right decision Warts-and-all communications to retain trust and learn Mobilising the next generation of leaders	#48, #11 #49, #50, #12, #3 #51, #13, #52 #14
Corporate assets and resources	Intelligent finance to fund sustainability interventions Efficient use of resources from better estates management Smarter procurement through whole-life costing Effecting change through staff compliance and champions	#4, #15 #53, #54, #55, #56, #57, #58, #59, #16 #17, #18, #60, #61, #62, #19 #63, #64, #65, #20 ,#21
Economic development and planning	Adapting to climate change Establishing low-carbon trade zones to support jobs and skills Business support through incubation, signals and controls Valuing the green space infrastructure	#5, #66, #22 #23, #67 #68, #69, #70, #24 #71, #25
Waste and environmental services	Valuing the asset at the bottom of the bin Increasing waste reduction Increasing the repair and re-use of goods Increasing recycling	#72 #26, #73, #74, #75, #76, #77 #78, #27 #6, #28, #79, #29, #80
Fleet and logistics	Reducing emissions and improving health from employee commuting Reducing emissions and lowering operating costs from business travel Reducing emissions, improving health and tackling congestion from public travel	#30, #81 #82, # 83, #31, #84. #7, #85 #32, #33, #86, #34, #35, #36, #37, #87, #88
Community management	Localism and maintaining the vitality of neighbourhoods Nurturing role models in the community Improving education and well-being Promoting a sustainable domestic lifestyle	#38, #39, #40 #8, #89, #90 #91 ,#41, #42, #92, #93 #95, #96, #97, #43, #98, #99, #100, #101, #44, #102

You may be doing none, some or most of these already. Whichever way, it can be a handy tool to benchmark yourself, a guide to assure colleagues what is and what could be done, as well as to learn from others.

13.2 **From learning to mandating**

At the start of this book we talked about the different approaches you can take to changing behaviour (engaging, emoting, empowering and enforcing) and we have seen throughout the value associated with such a process, from the revolving fund for water in Nillumbik to stimulating green operations in Montgomery.

An appetite for ongoing, genuine and comprehensive learning from others is clearly helpful to success here. Take, for instance, a novel approach adopted in Växjö, Sweden.

[#45] Two-year education programme in Växjö, Sweden

A multi-year education programme was launched across the city government in Växjö to enable staff to better understand the sustainability agenda and provide a new, open, radical forum for idea generation (Forum for the Future 2010).

As a result of the successful education initiative, eco-driving lessons were funded for city government officers and the council's heating system was switched from oil to bioenergy.

As well as observing the value of engaging, emoting and empowering staff or residents you should also appreciate the power of enforcing action through mandatory interventions as espoused by Kyoto's and Tokyo's local authorities in terms of requirements on business to report on their carbon reduction plans (as detailed in Chapter 9). At the same time we need to heed the cautionary words of Ostrom (1990) in terms of effective CPRs (discussed in Chapter 12); thus mandatory interventions should only be used in an appropriate way.

So, what is a smart pathway to mandatory action, then? Figure 13.2 has a number of elementary steps to making it happen.

FIGURE 13.2 **Normalising sustainability actions within your council**

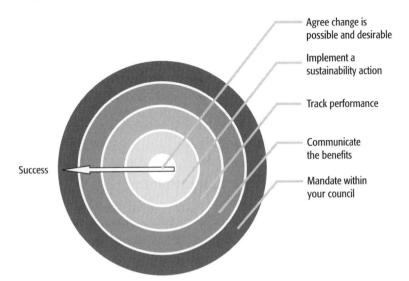

Agree change is possible and desirable

Implement a sustainability action

Track performance

Communicate the benefits

Mandate within your council

Success

As is evident from Figure 13.2, you need to start by gaining agreement that change is possible and desirable, then track and communicate success of the schemes once they are implemented. Then, communicate the benefits and, ultimately, request approval from the council's leadership to mandate the particular behaviour changes.

So, how about looking at a handful of your sustainability issues and consider and pilot one or two, maybe water conservation or green office operations as a start? (We explore how this fits in with your longer-term planning and how you can begin to take this forward in Chapters 14 and 15, respectively.)

Key learning

✓ An appetite for continued learning on sustainability innovations is vital in your efforts to battle back.

✓ Be clear on what, if anything, you want to become mandatory actions and why so.

14

Reaffirming what is meant by excellence

Where national governments are falling short, cities are taking action and achieving results (David Miller, Chair C40 Large Cities Climate Leadership Group, and Mayor of Toronto, 2008).

Typical sustainability actions and outcomes	Cost-neutral interventions
14.1 Excellence in austerity framework	#46
14.2 Systems alignment and integration	–

14.1 **Excellence in austerity framework**

So, given the insights on the actions and activities we have observed from local authorities around the world, what does excellence on sustainability look, sound and feel like in austere times?

As much as these cost-neutral opportunities can make a difference, one things is imperative: we must step up to the challenge and grasp this time with both hands. Now is the time for courage and you have a pivotal role to play if we are to save the planet during this turbulent moment in history.

This may require a slow and gentle approach for some of your colleagues or radical culture shift for others, but what is for certain is that five 'golden rules' must be observed here among leaders during austerity. This is depicted in Figure 14.1.

FIGURE 14.1 **Excellence in austerity framework**

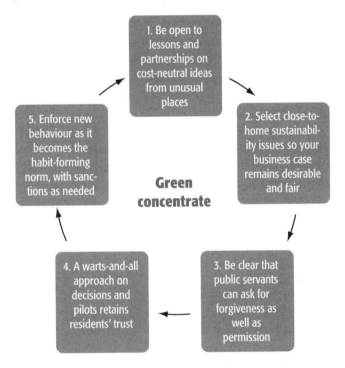

Thus, in order to secure real change, you need to understand how and when to engage, emote, empower or enforce. In essence, this describes a new paradigm for local government, what we can coin as **green concentrate**. By 'green concentrate' we mean: focused, cost-neutral interventions on sustainability during a time of *reduced* spending, made possible by *freezing* choices to enforce positive changes.

Just as important as practical steps, though, is that you have mapped a long-term plan for taking action on your priority issues. Take a look at what Vancouver is doing, for inspiration.

[#46] **A 100-year plan in Vancouver, Canada**

The forward-thinking council of Vancouver has developed a 100-year plan for sustainability (Grist 2007). Compare this long-term vision to the length of normal plans, which range from five to ten years, and the difference is amazing.

Early actions have included drawing 90% of its power from renewable sources in the form of hydroelectric, with solar, wind, wave and tidal energy to follow.

To illustrate the point further, returning to the smarter-driving example from the UK's Knowsley Council, we saw how such an initiative could take the form of refreshing employee job descriptions (so it is a mandatory requirement for all fleet staff to adopt smarter-driving) with repeated failure to drive in a smart way resulting in sanctions.

Remember, this is not the first time local leaders have been tasked with solving some of the greatest challenges posed to humankind in austere times. Think again about the renaissance of the USA following the first great depression or the reconstruction of Europe following the defeat of the Nazis in the Second World War.

The resilience of the human spirit knows no bounds. So, we are well placed to do it again, and revitalise our livelihoods. Indeed, working with your local communities is the perfect place to start as they are the heartbeat of humankind.

14.2 **Systems alignment and integration**

From the outset of this book we have stressed the importance of taking action on sustainability matters in a way that supports and informs your council's core strategy, but also integrates with how you do everyday business from an operational perspective. This is the same whether it is domestic waste segregation in Krakow or office energy consumption in Caracas.

Consequently, in Figure 14.2.1, the outline of a 'management dashboard' is proposed. (By dashboard, we mean a set of indicators and

FIGURE 14.2.1 **Management dashboard**

Financial

- Cost-neutral interventions only, with a payback period of five years or less (e.g. revolving fund for water conservation)

- Opportunity to make savings or generate new inward investment (e.g. greener buildings that consume less energy or special economic zones)

- Help to future-proof council against medium- to long-term public sector cuts (e.g. 'self-help' mantra of many of interventions so you can begin to manage down residents' expectations about service delivery)

Internal processes

- Business case for taking action on sustainability matters aligned to core strategy and operations of council (e.g. compliance with environmental law and primary duty of care to protect local residents)

- Positive governance as a 'practise what you preach' approach with service-led interventions (i.e. democratic services, corporate assets and resources)

- Natural synergies for integrated management of material risks with ISO 9000 and 14001 standards (plan, do, check, act) and Six Sigma (defining, measuring, analysing, improving, controlling)

Customer

- People-centric interventions, selected on the basis that are desirable among council residents as well as high-impact (e.g. green space events that are fun, healthy and support community cohesion through inter-generational play)

- Doing more for less is better value for money for local taxpayers and central government sponsor departments. Supported by hard data on need and performance metrics (e.g. increase in $ efficiency savings reduction in CO_2 emissions, better rates of satisfaction)

Learning and growth

- Supports a culture of learning among council officers and members by identifying new solutions to old problems from piloting and networking

- The 4 Es of behaviour change (engage, emote, empower, enforce) provide a path for mandating positive changes (e.g. amending job descriptions of fleet staff to drive smarter)

- 'Bouncing back' ethos ensures stakeholders inside and outside of council remain enthusiastic, productive and satisfied during a period of significant spending cuts, change and transition controls to allow you to drive in the right direction, similar to a motor vehicle.) This can be used as your template for setting up and operating your cost-neutral interventions.

So, think about how your sustainability planning interfaces with other corporate planning tools and standards, whether a balanced scorecard or the ISO standards.

The management dashboard in Figure 14.2.1 demonstrates this point and draws on generic guidelines set out by the architects of the balanced scorecard, Kaplan and Norton (2006), as well as elements of Six Sigma (Brue 2002) and the ISO series of standards such as ISO 9000, 14001 and 26000 related to quality management, environmental management and corporate social responsibility, respectively.

To demonstrate how this might work in practice for you, Figure 14.2.2 takes the example of business travel and works it through on the scorecard. As you can see, measures range from those that relate to the finance domain (i.e. $ savings from reduced fuel consumption) to internal processes (i.e. staff training and incentives to drive smarter).

Key learning

✓ Excellence in austerity for local government is about understanding how and when to engage, emote, empower or enforce on close-to-home, cost-neutral, sustainability issues.

✓ Key is that you align your approach to core business planning processes, because it is all about **green concentrate** – focused interventions during a time of *reduced* spending made possible by *freezing* choices to enforce positive changes.

FIGURE 14.2.2 **Scorecard for business travel**

15

Over to you

All through the ages the African people have made efforts to deliver themselves from oppressive forces. It is important that a critical mass of Africans do not accept the verdict that the world tries to push down their throat so as to give up and succumb. The struggle must continue. It is important to nurture any new ideas and initiatives which can make a difference for Africa (Wangari Maathai, Nobel Peace Prize Winner, Kenya 1995).

Typical sustainability actions and outcomes	Cost-neutral interventions
15.1 Kick-starting the use of your new learning	#47
15.2 Phased change: From trials to embedding	—

15.1 Kick-starting the use of your new learning

In the Preface to this book we began with a number of high-level questions we sought to answer: why is it fundamentally important for leaders in local government to 'play to win' when it comes to sustainability? And what practical action can councils take to implement national policies at a time when budgets are being savagely cut, the need to improve sustainability performance is ever more urgent and yet public appetite for change is on the wane?

As you will now know, we have provided the answers to these questions and more besides!

So, where do you begin in taking all this new learning forward? Why not start with selecting your 'top ten' proposed interventions? This could involve selecting one or two actions for each of the service areas covered in Chapters 7 and 12, in order to secure cross-council department interest.

To get your governance process right it must be supported by a long-term plan, with a vision, perhaps like that of Chicago, below.

[#47] **Race to the top in Chicago, USA**

Chicago is striving to make itself 'the greenest city in America' (Grist 2007). This includes cost-neutral schemes such as building some of the most ecologically friendly municipal buildings in the country, providing incentives for homeowners to be more energy-efficient and helping low-income families get solar power.

This complements wider work including the planting of 500,000 new trees, investing hundreds of millions of dollars in the revitalisation of parks and neighbourhoods and adding more than 2 million square feet of rooftop gardens—more than all other US cities combined.

15.2 **Phased change: from trials to embedding**

You will recall that moving this forward will not only need a vision (as ground-breaking as that of Chicago or not) but also involve you preparing a robust business case 'pitch' in such a way that it can deal with the most 'hard-nosed' of sceptics. So, a phased approach to implementation over a number of years is preferable, as proposed in Figure 15.2. Remember: after all, it is about **green concentrate**—grappling with the big issues ranging from keeping money local to climate adaptation while operating on reduced budgets—and you therefore need to have a measured, forward-looking approach over a number of years.

FIGURE 15.2 **Where to start: developing a forward-thinking approach**

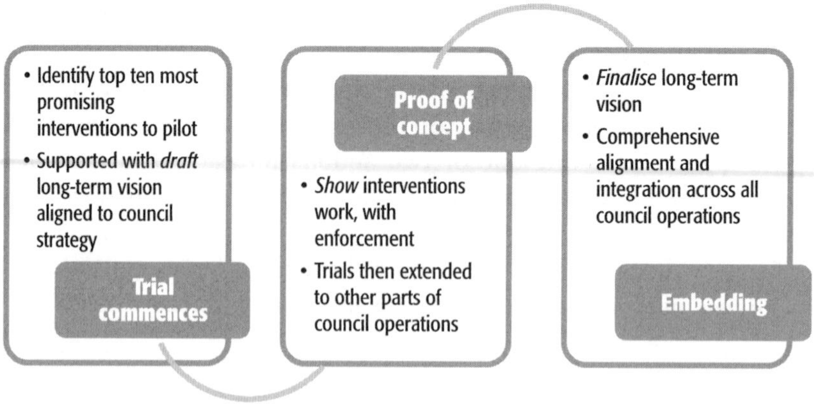

- Identify top ten most promising interventions to pilot
- Supported with *draft* long-term vision aligned to council strategy

Trial commences

Proof of concept

- *Show* interventions work, with enforcement
- Trials then extended to other parts of council operations

- *Finalise* long-term vision
- Comprehensive alignment and integration across all council operations

Embedding

As you can see from all the inspiring stories from Caracas to Ekurhuleni, Fort Chipewyan to Krakow, Knowsley to Montgomery, and Nillumbik to Ulaanbaatar, using all our intelligence and tremendous grit we can battle back and take 'game-changing' action on sustainable matters, even as we emerge from a terrifying global recession.

It is a great challenge we face as leaders in local government, but we are more than capable of making it happen. Do you have enough determination and dedication?

If yes, then now it is over to you and your inspiring leadership to save the planet, starting with your council!

Key learning

✓ Start with your 'top ten' most appealing interventions, as part of a wider, long-term vision or plan.

✓ Remember: your contribution is vital; you can make a big difference on **green concentrate**, but we need to work together.

Abbreviations

BREEAM	BRE Environmental Assessment Method
CO_2	carbon dioxide
CHP	combined heat and power
CNG	concentrated natural gas
CPRs	common pool resources
EMS	environmental management system
EST	Energy Saving Trust
EU	European Union
FAO	Food and Agriculture Organisation
GHG	greenhouse gas emissions
GMT	Greenwich Mean Time
GRI	Global Reporting Initiative
GSHP	ground source heat pumps
GWP	greenhouse warming potential
HGV	heavy goods vehicle
IPCC	Intergovernmental Panel on Climate Change
ISO	International Organisation for Standardisation
LED	light-emitting diode
LEED	Leadership in Energy and Environmental Design
LPG	liquefied petroleum gas
MDGs	Millennium Development Goals
MPG	miles per gallon
NGO	non-governmental organisation
NO_x	nitrogen oxide (NO) or nitrogen dioxide (NO_2)
PAYS	pay as you save

PV   photovoltaic
SO_x sulphur oxide (SO) or sulphur dioxide (SO_2)
SWH   solar water heating
UNEP   United Nations Environment Programme
WBCSD   World Business Council for Sustainable Development
WRI   World Resources Institute

Units of measurement

gCO_2/km   grams of carbon dioxide per kilometre
ha   hectares (of bio-productive land)
kg   kilogram
$kgCO_2$ kilograms of carbon dioxide
mph   miles per hour
rpm   revolutions per minute
tCO_2e tonnes of carbon dioxide equivalent
tCO_2/t product   tonnes of carbon dioxide per tonne of (food) product
°C   degrees Celsius (temperature)

Bibliography

10:10 (2010) 'Lighter Later', www.lighterlater.org, accessed April 2010.

AccountAbility and UNEP (2010) *Climate Change Competitiveness Index* (London: AccountAbility).

APSE (Association for Public Service Excellence) (2009) *Driving Better Value From Your Fleet* (London: OGC).

Bendell, J., and J. Cohen (2009) 'World Review', *Journal of Corporate Citizenship* 27: 6-17.

Borg, J. (2007) *Persuasion: The Art of Influencing People* (London: Prentice Hall).

Boulding, K. (1966) 'The Economics of the Coming Spaceship Earth', in H. Daly and K. Townsend (eds.), *Valuing the Earth: Economics, Ecology, Ethics* (New York: Harper Collins): 297-310.

Bouthier, A. (2010) 'Japan Mayor Hopes to Make History with Milk Bottle, Nappies', www.independent.co.uk/life-style/house-and-home/japan-mayor-hopes-to-make-history-with-milk-bottle-nappies-1920742.html, accessed 30 September 2010.

Boyle, D. (2009) *Localism: Unravelling the Supplicant State* (London: New Economics Foundation).

Branigan, T. (2010) 'Winter of "white death" killed 10m livestock—and nomad's way of life', *The Guardian*, 20 July 2010: 21.

BRE (Building Research Establishment) (1994) *Low Energy Domestic Lighting* (Watford, UK: BRE).

Brown, L. (2009) *Plan B 4.0: Mobilizing to Save Civilization* (Washington, DC: Earth Policy Institute).

Brue, G. (2002) *Six Sigma for Managers* (Maidenhead, UK: McGraw-Hill).

CADDET (Centre for the Analysis and Dissemination of Demonstrated Energy Technologies) (1995) *Learning from Experiences with Advanced Houses of the World* (Sittard, Netherlands: CADDET).

Caldwell, W. (2008) *A Roadmap from Conflict to Peace* (Washington, DC: Centre for Strategic and International Studies).

Carrington, D. (2010) 'Eat Insects to Save the World, Says Food Expert', *The Observer*, 1 August 2010: 16.

CIBSE (Chartered Institution of Building Services Engineers) (2006) *Guide A: Environmental Design* (London: CIBSE).

Civitas (2010) *Move: The Civitas Initiative Quarterly Newsletter* 3 (April 2010).

DCLG (Department of Communities and Local Government) (2006) *A Guide to Sustainability of Existing Buildings: Energy Efficiency of Dwellings—Initial Analysis* (London: DCLG).

De Montfort University (2010) *Energy in Buildings* (Leicester, UK: De Montfort University).

DECC (Department of Energy and Climate Change) (2009) *UK Low Carbon Transition Plan* (London: HM Government).

Defra (Department for Environment, Food and Rural Affairs) (2010) 'NI188 Adapting to Climate Change', www.defra.gov.uk, accessed May 2010.

Department for Transport (2009) *A Carbon Reduction Strategy for Transport, UK* (London: Department for Transport).

Doppelt, B. (2010) *Leading Change Toward Sustainability: A Change-Management Guide for Business, Government and Civil Society* (Sheffield, UK: Greenleaf Publishing).

Du Plessis, A., E. Le Roux, W. Bluemer and J. Lommen (2004) *Greener Governance in Southern SADC: Success Report on Medium Sized Local Authorities* (Potchefstroom, South Africa: Centre for Environmental Management, North-West University; Enschede, Netherlands: Saxion Hogeschool).

East, R. (2004) 'Where Mayors Mean Most', *Green Futures*, 9 June 2004 (www.forumforthefuture.org/greenfutures/articles/601875).

Ehrenfeld, J. (2010) *Sustainability by Design: A Subversive Strategy for Transforming Our Consumer Culture* (London: Yale University Press).

The Environmentalist (2010) 'Recycling Still the Most Effective Waste Disposal Method', *The Environmentalist* 95: 5.

EST (Energy Saving Trust) (2008) *Media Fact Sheet 2008–09* (London: EST).

Ethical Corporation (2009) *Marks & Spencer's A-grade Progress* (London: Ethical Corporation).

European Commission (2010) 'Youth Parliament of Oslo', ec.europa.eu/youth/sharing-experience/experience1249_en.htm, accessed 30 September 2010.

European Conference of Ministers for Transport (2004) 'How we compare with the rest of Europe', *The Guardian*, April 2010: 17-18.

Feng, A., and A. Sauer (2004) *Comparison of Passenger Fuel Economy and Greenhouse Gas Emission Standards around the World* (Washington, DC: Pew Center on Global Climate Change).

Forstater, M., J. Oelschaegel, M. Sillanpää and E. Mayo (2006) *What Assures Consumers?* (London: AccountAbility/National Consumer Council).

——, J. Oelschaegel and R. Lloyd (2007) *What Assures Consumers on Climate Change?* (London: AccountAbility/Consumers International).

Forum for the Future (2009a) *The Sustainable Cities Index: Rating the Largest 20 British Cities* (London: Forum for the Future).

—— (2009b) *Smarter Finance: How to Get More Carbon Savings for Your Cash* (London: Forum for the Future).

—— (2010) *Stepping Up: A Framework for Public Sector Leadership on Sustainability* (London: Forum for the Future).

Global Compact Cities Programme (2010) *Sustainable Cities* (Volume 1; Melbourne: RMIT University).

Goldenberg, S. (2010) 'Eco-warriors: US Navy Plans for a Greener Fighting Force', *The Guardian*, 21 April 2010: 5.

Gore, J., and J. Hodgson (2010) 'Managing the Climate Change Message', *The Environmentalist* 96 (19 April 2010).

Gray, L. (2009) 'Obama's Green Guru Calls for White Roofs', *The Telegraph*, 27 May 2009 (www.telegraph.co.uk/earth/earthnews/5389278/Obamas-green-guru-calls-for-white-roofs.html).

Grayling, A.C. (2007) *Towards the Light: The Story of the Struggles for Liberty and Rights that Made the Modern West* (Cranleigh, UK: Midas).

Green Scissors (2010) 'Cutting Wasteful and Environmentally Harmful Spending', www.greenscissors.com, accessed May 2010.

Greenpeace (2010) *Make IT Green: Cloud Computing and its Contribution to Climate Change* (Washington, DC: Greenpeace)

Grist (2007) '15 Green Cities', www.grist.org/article/cities/3, accessed May 2010.

Hartwick, J. (1977) 'Intergenerational Equity and the Investing of Rents from Exhaustible Resources', *American Economic Review* 67: 972-74.

Heath, C., and D. Heath (2007) *Made to Stick: Why Some Ideas Survive and Others Die* (New York: Random House).

Howarth, L. (2010) 'Roof Tiles to Cool the Planet', *Green Futures*, 2 February 2010 (www.forumforthefuture.org/greenfutures/articles/Roof_tiles_cool_planet).

IPCC (Intergovernmental Panel on Climate Change) (2007) *Climate Change 2007: Fourth Assessment Report* (Geneva: IPCC).

Jackson, T. (2009) *Prosperity without Growth: Economics for a Finite Planet* (London: Earthscan).

Jowett, J. (2010) 'World Leaders Call For Global Water Price Rise', *The Guardian*, 28 April 2010: 20.

Kaplan, R., and D. Norton (2006) *Alignment: Using the Balanced Scorecard to Create Corporate Synergies* (Boston, MA: Harvard Business School Press).

LGA (Local Government Association) (2009) *The Climate Challenge: Local Solutions through Global Learning* (London: LGA).

Mayo, E., and A. Nairn (2009) *Consumer Kids: How Big Business is Grooming our Children for Profit* (London: Constable & Robinson).

McKibben, B. (2010) *Deep Economy: Economics as if the World Mattered* (Oxford, UK: Oneworld Publications).

McKie, R. (2010) 'The Emails Affairs and my Problem with Climate Deniers', *The Observer*, 18 May 2010: 14-15.

McMullan, R. (2007) *Environmental Science in Building* (Basingstoke, UK: Palgrave Macmillan, 6th edn).

Monaghan, P., BSR and J. Weiser (2003) *Business and Economic Development: The Impact of Corporate Responsibility Standards and Practices* (London: AccountAbility; San Francisco: Business for Social Responsibility; Branford, CT: Brody Weiser Burns).

Monbiot, G. (2006) *Heat: How to Stop the Planet Burning* (London: Allen Lane).

Mukherjee, S. (2009) 'Village Aims to Kick Carbon Habit', BBC News, news.bbc.co.uk/1/hi/sci/tech/8152579.stm, accessed 30 September 2010.

National Consumer Council and Sustainable Development Commission (2009) *I Will if you Will: Towards Sustainable Consumption* (London: National Consumer Council/Sustainable Development Commission).

Natural England (2009) *The Economic Value of Green Infrastructure* (Sheffield, UK: Natural England).

North East Lincolnshire Council (2009) *Carbon Management Plan* (Grimsby, UK: North East Lincolnshire Council).

NWDA (Northwest Regional Development Agency) (2009) 'Manchester Region to become Built Environment in Low Carbon Economic Area', press release, www.nwda.co.uk/news--events/press-releases/200901/gtr-mcr-lcea-built-environment.aspx, accessed 10 September 2010).

O'Hara, G. (2010) 'How (not) to Cut Government Spending and Reduce Public Sector Debt', History & Policy, www.historyandpolicy.org/papers/policy-paper-95.html, accessed 10 September 2010.

OGC (Office of Government Commerce) (2007) *Local Government Sustainability Procurement Strategy* (London: Cabinet Office).

Ostrom, E. (1990) *Governing the Commons: The Evolution of Institutions for Collective Action* (New York: Cambridge University Press).

Parfitt, J. (2002) *Waste Not, Want Not* (Banbury, UK: WRAP).

Perman, R., M. Yue, J. McGilvray and M. Common (2003) *Natural Resource and Environmental Economics* (Harlow, UK: Pearson).

Porritt, J. (2007) *Capitalism as if the World Matters* (London: Earthscan).

Power, A., and J. Houghton (2007) *Jigsaw Cities: Big Places, Small Spaces* (Bristol, UK: The Policy Press).

Rawls, J. (1971) *A Theory of Justice* (Cambridge, MA: Harvard University Press).

Responsible Purchasing Network (2010) 'Green 101: Best Practices', Center for a New American Dream, www.responsiblepurchasing.org/purchasing_guides/all/practices, accessed April 2010.

Rubbens, C., P. Monaghan, E. Bonfiglioli and S. Zadek (2002) *Impacts of Reporting: The Role of Social and Sustainability Reporting in Organisational Transformation* (London: AccountAbility; Brussels: CSR Europe).

Satterthwaite, D. (2009) 'The Implications of Population Growth and Urbanization for Climate Change', *Environment & Urbanization* 21: 545-67.

Serventi, E. (2010) 'New Dispensers Cut Packaging by 96.3%', *Green Futures*, 31 March 2010 (www.forumforthefuture.org/greenfutures/articles/New_dispensers_cut_packaging+).

Sherman, J. (2007) 'Pay-As-You-Throw Scheme for Waste "Penalises Householders"', *The Times*, 25 May 2007 (www.timesonline.co.uk/tol/news/politics/article1837982.ece).

Shermer, M., D. MacKenzie, R. Littlemore, J. Giles and M. Fitzpatrick (2010) 'Living in Denial', *New Scientist* 2,760 (Special Report): 35-44.

Social Investment Forum (2009) 'Socially Responsible Investors, Labor, Pension Funds Agree: Bail-out Recipients Facing Say-on-Pay Resolutions Should Adopt Policy', press release, www.socialinvest.org/news/releases/pressrelease.cfm?id=133, accessed 30 September 2010.

Soriaga, R. (2008) *Strengthening Landscape Alliances to Secure Environmental Services* (Bohol, Philippines: Asia Forest Network).

State of Michigan (2010) 'Michigan Meatout Day', www.michigan.gov/gov/0,1607,7-168-25488_54480-232493-,00.html, accessed 30 September 2010.

Stern, N. (2006) *Stern Review on the Economics of Climate Change* (London: HM Treasury).

UNFCCC (UN Framework Convention on Climate Change) (2010) *Report of the Conference of Parties on its Fifteenth Session*, Copenhagen, 7–19 December 2009.

United Nations (2009) *The Millennium Development Goals Report* (New York: UN).

United Nations Commission on Sustainable Development (1994) *Oslo Roundtable on Sustainable Production and Consumption* (New York: UN CSD).

US Department of Energy (2010) 'Office of Electricity Delivery and Energy Reliability', www.oe.energy.gov, accessed March 2010.

Vale, R. (2009) *Time to Eat the Dog* (London: Thames & Hudson).

Vaughan, A. (2010) 'Sustainable fishing move could help your cat reduce its eco pawprint', *The Guardian*, 31 March 2010.

Vaze, P. (2009) *The Economical Environmentalist* (London: Earthscan).

Vitali Energy (2007) *Owners Handbook, ING Real Estate and Carillion* (Manchester: Vitali Energy).

Wakefield Council (2009) *Sustainable Procurement Case Study* (Wakefield, UK: Wakefield Council).

Walker, P. (2010) 'Help Your Skin, Your Figure, Your Bank Balance and the Planet' *The Environmentalist* 95: 10-11.

WBCSD (World Business Council for Sustainable Development) (2008) *Sustainable Consumption Facts and Trends* (Geneva: WBCSD).

WCED (World Commission on Environment and Development) (1987) *Our Common Future* (Oxford, UK: Oxford University Press).

We Are What We Do (2007) *Change the World for a Fiver* (London: Short Books).

Weiser, J., and S. Zadek (2000) *Conversations with Disbelievers: Persuading Companies to Address Social Changes* (New York: Ford Foundation).

Welford, R. (1997) *Corporate Environmental Management* (London: Earthscan).

Wire, T. (2009) *Fewer Emitters, Lower Emissions, Less Costs: Reducing Future Carbon Emissions by Investing in Family Planning, A Cost–Benefit Analysis* (London: London School of Economics).

WWF (2006) *Living Planet Report* (Gland, Switzerland: WWF).

Yarrow, J. (2008) *How to Reduce Your Carbon Footprint: 365 Ways to Make a Real Difference* (London: Duncan Baird Publishers).

Zadek, S., and M. Merme (2003) *Redefining Materiality* (London: AccountAbility/UK Social Investment Forum).

About the author

Philip Monaghan is a recognised and highly successful leader with over 16 years of experience as a strategist and change manager in the fields of economic development and environmental sustainability across the public, non-profit and private sectors.

An accomplished public speaker and writer on such matters, he has featured as an expert for television and newspapers including for the BBC and the *Financial Times*. Philip has a degree in economics and is presently reading an MSc in Climate Change and Sustainable Development. He is a member of the Institute of Environmental Management & Assessment (IEMA) and in 2007 was also elected as a Fellow of the Royal Society for the Encouragement of Arts, Manufactures and Commerce (RSA) in recognition of his work to date.

Presently, Philip is Head of Environmental Sustainability for Knowsley Metropolitan Borough Council, part of the Liverpool City Region in the UK. His team leads on the coordination and delivery of council-wide actions on climate change, environmental behaviour change such as waste minimisation, green spaces, environmental management systems and sustainable development.

Prior to this he worked for the world-renowned think-tank Account-Ability for five years in numerous senior management roles. Before this he spent nearly a decade with professional service providers WSP Group (a global engineering consultancy), The National Centre for Business and Sustainability, and PS EPEC (PS Economic, Planning and Environmental Consultants). This is in addition to assignments with North East Lincolnshire Council, Groundwork (an environmental charity) and Consumer Focus (a consumer advocacy body).

During his career Philip has worked with an array of partners and clients across mainland Europe and in Hong Kong, Japan, Peru, Russia, South Africa, USA and Venezuela, including with the European Commission, the UK Department for Business, Innovation and Skills (BIS), the United Nations Environment Programme (UNEP), WWF, Gap Inc, Marks & Spencer and Vodafone.

From 2011 Philip takes up a new role as a guest lecturer at the University of Liverpool, in the School of Environmental Sciences.

Other articles and publications he has co-authored include: *What Assures Consumers on Climate Change?* (2007, AccountAbility and Consumers International); *Food Labelling: Understanding Consumers Attitudes and Behaviour* (2007, Ashridge); *What Assures Consumers?* (2006, AccountAbility and National Consumers Council); *Putting the 'Corporate' Back into Corporate Responsibility* (2005, AccountAbility Forum); *Business and Economic Development* (2003, AccountAbility and BSR); *Impacts of Reporting* (2002, CSR Europe and AccountAbility); and *Sustainable Banking* (2001, Greenleaf Publishing).

Philip can be contacted at sustainabilityinausterity.wordpress.com.

Other helpful sources of learning

Local government networks

- **APSE: Association for Public Service Excellence** is a not-for-profit specialist in local authority front-line services in areas ranging from environmental services to housing
  www.apse.org.uk

- **C40 Cities**: a group of large cities committed to tackling climate change through effective partnership working with the Clinton Climate Initiative
  www.c40cities.org

- **Covenant of Mayors**: a commitment by signatory towns and cities to go beyond the objectives of EU energy policy in terms of reduction in CO_2 emissions
  www.eumayors.eu

- **ICLEI: Local Governments for Sustainability** is an international association of local governments and their associations that have made a commitment to sustainable development
  www.iclei.org

- **LGA**: the Local Government Association lobbies and campaigns for changes in policy, legislation and funding on behalf of our councils and the people and communities they serve
  www.lga.gov.uk

- **Low Carbon Innovation Network**: a best practice exchange for organisations to progress their plans for carbon-reduction initiatives
  www.carbon-innovation.com

- **UN Global Compact Cities Programme**: the urban component of the United Nations Global Compact initiative. The Programme's international secretariat is located at RMIT University in Melbourne, Australia
  www.citiesprogramme.org

Intergovernmental organisations

- **FAO**: the Food and Agriculture Organisation of the United Nations leads international efforts to defeat hunger
  www.fao.org

- **IPCC**: the Intergovernmental Panel on Climate Change is the leading body for the assessment of climate change, established by the United Nations Environment Programme
  www.ipcc.ch

- **International Energy Agency**: an intergovernmental organisation which acts as energy policy adviser to countries in their effort to ensure reliable, affordable and clean energy
  www.iea.org

- **UNDP**: the United Nations Development Programme aims to build effective and capable states that are accountable and transparent, inclusive and responsive
  www.undp.org

- **UNEP**: the United Nations Environment Programme provides leadership and encourages partnership in caring for the environment by inspiring, informing and enabling nations and people to improve their quality of life
  www.unep.org

Non-governmental organisations

- **AccountAbility**: a global non-profit organisation that works to promote accountability innovations for sustainable development
  www.accountability21.net

- **Asia Forest Network**: dedicated to supporting the role of communities in protection and sustainable use of Asia's forests
  www.asiaforestnetwork.org

- **Eco-Schools**: a programme for environmental management and certification, designed to implement sustainable development education in schools
  www.eco-schools.org

- **Fah Diow Foundation**: working in Thailand to give all sectors of society a voice in creating a future that is more fair, and more environmentally and socially responsible than is currently the case
  www.fahdiow.net

- **FoodShare**: a non-profit community organisation whose vision is 'Good Healthy Food for All' from growing and distribution of food to its purchasing and consumption
  www.foodshare.net

- **Forum for the Future**: an independent, non-profit organisation with a mission to promote sustainable development
  www.forumforthefuture.org

- **Greenpeace**: a global campaigning organisation that seeks to protect the natural environment and promote peace
  www.greenpeace.org

- **The Center for a New American Dream**: set up to help Americans consume responsibly to protect the environment, enhance quality of life and promote social justice
  www.newdream.org

- **WWF**: the mission is to stop the degradation of the planet's natural environment and to build a future in which humans live in harmony with nature.
  wwf.panda.org

- **10:10**: a project to unite every sector of society behind one simple idea—we all commit to reduce our emissions by 10% in 2010, then work together to make it happen
  www.1010global.org

Academic, research or professional institutions

- **De Montfort University**: the Institute of Energy and Sustainable Development aims to create the knowledge necessary to achieve more energy-efficient and sustainable lifestyles
  www.dmu.ac.uk

- **Earth Policy Institute**: an international think-tank providing a vision of an environmentally sustainable economy
  www.earthpolicy.org

- **GRI**: the Global Reporting Initiative pioneers the development of the world's most widely used sustainability reporting framework
  www.globalreporting.org

- **IEMA**: the Institute of Environmental Management & Assessment promotes best practice standards in environmental management, auditing and assessment
  www.iema.net

- **Korean Research Institute for Human Settlements**: conducts studies on environment, regional economies, land research, construction, urban studies and infrastructure
  www.krihs.re.kr

- **North-West University**: Centre for Environmental Management delivers expertise and conducts research in environmental, safety and health management and related fields
  www.nwu.ac.za

- **Pew Center**: provides credible information, straight answers and innovative solutions in the effort to address global climate change
  www.pewclimate.org

- **RSA**: the Royal Society for the Encouragement of Art, Manufactures and Commerce seeks to develop and promote new ways of thinking about human fulfilment and social progress
www.thersa.org

- **University of Pretoria**: the Centre for Leadership aims to harness academic disciplines cutting across areas such as economics, natural sciences and humanities
web.up.ac.za

- **Water Footprint Network**: promotes the transition towards sustainable, fair and efficient use of freshwater resources
www.waterfootprint.org

- **World Resources Institute**: an environmental think-tank that goes beyond research to find practical ways to protect the Earth and improve people's lives
www.wri.org

Business networks

- **Business for Social Responsibility**: a global non-profit whose mission is to work with business to create a just and sustainable world
www.bsr.org

- **CSR Europe**: a network for business to share best practice on corporate social responsibility
www.csreurope.org

- **World Business Council for Sustainable Development**: aims to provide business leadership as a catalyst for change towards sustainable development
www.wbcsd.org

Green buildings

- **AECB**: the sustainable building association aims to promote standards and advice on the sustainable performance of buildings, constructed and refurbished
  www.aecb.net

- **iiSBE**: the International Initiative for a Sustainable Built Environment promotes best practice on building performance
  www.iisbe.org

- **SBIC**: the Sustainable Buildings Industry Council aims to unite and inspire the building industry towards higher performance through education and the mutual exchange of ideas
  www.sbicouncil.org

- **Sustainable Building Support Centre**: an intermediate organisation that organises activities to promote and develop sustainable building
  www.sustainablebuilding.info

Sustainable procurement

- **Consumers International**: the world federation of consumer groups that serves as the independent and authoritative global voice for consumers
  www.consumersinternational.org

- **Ethical Consumer Research Association**: a leading alternative consumer organisation that researches the social and environmental records of companies
  www.ethicalconsumer.org

- **FLO**: Fairtrade Labelling Organizations International coordinates fairtrade labelling at an international level
  www.fairtrade.net

- **Marine Stewardship Council**: develops standards for sustainable fishing and seafood traceability
  www.msc.org

- **Responsible Purchasing Network**: an international network of buyers dedicated to socially responsible and environmentally sustainable purchasing
www.responsiblepurchasing.org

Renewable energy

- **American Solar Energy Society**: aims to inspire an era of energy innovation and speed the transition to a sustainable energy economy
www.ases.org

- **Centre for Alternative Technology**: concerned with the search for globally sustainable, whole and ecologically sound technologies and ways of life
www.cat.org.uk

- **European Wind Energy Association**: the voice of the wind industry, actively promoting the utilisation of wind power in Europe and worldwide
www.ewea.org

- **SolarAid**: an international charity that develops local renewables solutions to tackle climate change and poverty
solar-aid.org

Note: all websites accessed September 2010

Index